RANDAL HENRY

BLACK FIRSTS

IN LOS ANGELES

RANDAL HENRY

BLACK FIRSTS

IN LOS ANGELES

GO CRENSHAW

The Crenshaw District, Los Angeles

Summary:

Black Firsts in Los Angeles shines a spotlight on more than 200 extraordinary achievements by Black Angelenos.

Notice:

The information in this book, referenced from available sources, is true to the best of our knowledge. However, the author and Go Crenshaw Publications disclaims all liability in connection with the use of this book.

First Printing 2024

ISBN 978-1-7361888-9-7 (hardcover)
ISBN 979-8-9875837-0-8 (paperback)

Published by Go Crenshaw Publications
The Crenshaw District, Los Angeles, CA
www.gocrenshaw.com | www.gocrenshaw.shop

▌ DEDICATION

This book is dedicated to Black Angelenos who never had the opportunity to be the first at anything. It's also dedicated to those whose pathway towards opportunity was stifled or filled with stumbling blocks and those whose achievements have gone unnoticed, undocumented, unheralded and underappreciated.

TABLE OF CONTENTS

PREFACE

Black Firsts in Los Angeles documents the accomplishments of Black Angelenos and stands as a testament to their extraordinary achievements, especially those that occurred after Los Angeles became part of the United States (U.S.). After writing *Black Firsts* I realized that, when it comes to Black achievement in Los Angeles, there are essentially three epochs: (1) the Spanish Colonial; (2) the Mexican Republic; and, (3) the United States. Relatively speaking, things in Los Angeles weren't all that bad for Black Angelenos during the colonial period when we were subjects of the Spanish empire (e.g., no large plantations, many free Black people, some Black soldiers, able to bear arms, able to own land, able to marry interracially, etc.). For example, in 1781, twenty-six free Black/Afro-Latinos, not only helped found the city, they held deed to property making them both LA's founding fathers and first landowners. In 1793, the Viceroyalty of New Spain (now Mexico) appointed Juan Francisco Reyes, a Black (Afro-Latino) man, Mayor (alcalde) of Los Angeles. During the Mexican period (i.e., 1821–1848), even greater opportunities existed for Black Angelenos. For instance, in 1829 slavery was abolished in Mexico when Vicente Ramon Guerrero, one of the leading revolutionary generals of the Mexican War of Independence against Spain, was elected as the first, and so far only, Black/Afro-Latino President of Mexico. That same year, Guerrero prohibited slavery in all of Mexico except in the Isthmus of Tehuantepec. In 1845, Pio Pico, a Black (Afro-Latino) man was elected Governor of California. In the same year, William Alexander Leidesdorff Jr, a Black man from the Dutch West Indies and a prominent citizen of Mexico, accepted a request to serve as the US Vice Consul to Mexico.

However, notwithstanding the amazing accomplishments highlighted in this book, beginning with the U.S. declaration of war on Mexico in 1846, the U.S. military invasion and occupation of Mexican Los Angeles in 1846/1847, the end of the U.S./Mexican war in 1848, through the Compromise of 1850 and California statehood, the opportunities that were afforded Black Angelenos as part of Spain and Mexico shrunk considerably when California came under U.S. jurisdiction.

INTRODUCTION

Black Firsts in Los Angeles details over 200 extraordinary, color-barrier breaking, achievements by Afro-Angelenos organized alphabetically into twenty-two chapters first by area of achievement (i.e, Architecture; Art; Aviation; Business; Civil Rights; Education; Engineering; Film, Television and Motion Pictures; Food; Government; Health; Journalism; Law; Library Science; Performing Arts; Public Service, Real Estate; Religion; Science; Sports; and, Transportation) and then chronologically.

Many of the "ground-breaking" events discussed in the book represent the first of their kind in the United States like the first Black aviators association, first Black flight school, first Black diplomat, and the first Black female to host her own television show, for example. Others represent Black firsts in the state of California like the first Black (Afro-Mexican) Governor; first Black Lieutenant Governor; first Black person elected to Congress from California; and, the first Black female licensed dentist in California. Still others represent Black firsts in the city of Los Angeles like the first Black newspaper; first Black lawyer; first Black policeman; first Black church; and, the first Black person on the housing commission.

The purpose of *Black Firsts in Los Angeles* is to (1) shine a spotlight on Black achievement, ingenuity, perseverance, resilience, and genius despite historical slavery, institutionalized racism, legalized discrimination, underfunded schools and subpar education opportunities, unfair housing and labor laws (e.g. redlining and last-hired/first fired), over-policing, "jim-crow" laws, and sundown towns to name just a few of the impediments that have prevented Black people from fully participating in American society; and (2) to provide a history of Black people in Los Angeles that is not included in school books or taught in classrooms.

Last, please note that, in this book the term "Black" and "Black People" is used to refer to people of African descent including Afro-Asians, Afro-Americans, Afro-Europeans, Afro-Hispanics, Afro-Indigenous, and Afro-Mexicans. And that, the terms "Black Angeleno" and "Afro-Angeleno" are used to refer to "Black" people who call Los Angeles, California home.

CHAP

HOLLYWOOD HILLS, 1928

SIDNEY
POITIER

LINCOLN
PERRY

ACTORS

■ FIRST BLACK MOVIE STAR IN HOLLYWOOD

Lincoln Perry was America's first Black movie star. Perry came to Los Angeles in the 1920s after a talent scout for Fox Studios offered him a screen test, which proved successful. In 1927, Perry, an actor, comedian and veteran of vaudeville's "Chitlin Circuit", got his big break when he was cast in the silent film In *Old Kentucky*. Perry created a character named "Stepin Fechit" whom many Americans thought of negatively. In the mid-1930s, Black leaders began putting pressure on Hollywood to rid the screen of the stereotype believing that "Stepin Fetchit" was keeping white America from viewing Black people as equals. While Perry achieved fame during his career, his legacy is complicated due to the racial stereotypes associated with his performances. It is important to understand the historical context and the evolving understanding of racial representation in media when discussing figures like Perry and their impact on popular culture. Perry died in 1985, at the age of 83 and was buried in Los Angeles. (B. 1902 – D. 1985)

■ FIRST BLACK PERFORMER TO WIN ACADEMY AWARD FOR BEST ACTOR

Sidney Poitier, whose Academy Award for the 1963 film *Lilies of the Field* made him the first Black performer to win in the best-actor category, rose to prominence when the civil rights movement was beginning to make headway in the United States. Poitier's portrayal of resolute heroes in films like *To Sir With Love*, *In the Heat of the Night* and *Guess Who's Coming to Dinner* established him as Hollywood's first Black matinee idol and helped open the door for Black actors in the film industry. Poitier's achievements as an actor and his involvement in the civil rights movement left an indelible mark on both the film industry and American society as a whole. Poitier died in his Los Angeles home in 2022 at the age of 94. (B. 1927 – D. 2022)

◼ FIRST BLACK ACTOR TO CO-STAR IN A TELEVISION WESTERN

In 1969, Otis Young became the first Black actor to co-star in a television Western series called The Outcasts. He played a former slave who became a bounty hunter. Young was an known for his role as Corporal "Doc" Greene in the television series which aired from 1968 to 1969. The Outcasts was a western series set in the Reconstruction Era after the American Civil War. In his role as Corporal Greene, Young became the first Black actor to co-star in a television western series.

This was a significant milestone in television history, as it broke barriers and provided representation for Black actors in a genre that had predominantly featured white actors up until that point. While the series was short-lived, lasting only one season, it made an important contribution to television by showcasing a Black actor in a leading role within the western genre. Young died in Los Angeles at the age of 69. (B. 1932 – D. 2001).

GHOST TOWN

OTIS YOUNG

EDNA
STEWART

NICK
STEWART

ACTORS THEATER

■ FIRST BLACK-OWNED ACTORS THEATER IN LOS ANGELES

Nick Stewart was an American actor, musician, and civil rights activist, best known for his role as Lightnin' on the radio and television show *Amos 'n' Andy*. Born on March 15, 1910, in New York City, Stewart began his career as a performer in vaudeville and later transitioned to film and television. In 1950, using their life's savings, Nick Stewart and his wife, Edna, organized the Ebony Showcase Theater with the mission of providing a space where Black actors could perform outside the usual media stereotypes. The Ebony Showcase Theater played a vital role in nurturing African American talent and fostering community engagement. Nick and Edna Stewart's dedication to promoting Black artists and their commitment to civil rights activism made them influential figures within the Black community and the entertainment industry. The Ebony Showcase's stage has been a crucible for hundreds of Black actors who moved on to film and television roles. Stewart said "Virtually every major Black star has interacted with the Ebony Showcase and knows its history."

The original theater building, located at 4718-26 W. Washington Blvd., was demolished in 1998 and replaced by the Nate Holden Performing Arts Center. Nick Stewart: (B. 1910 – D. 2000). Edna Stewart: (B. 1918 – D. 2022).

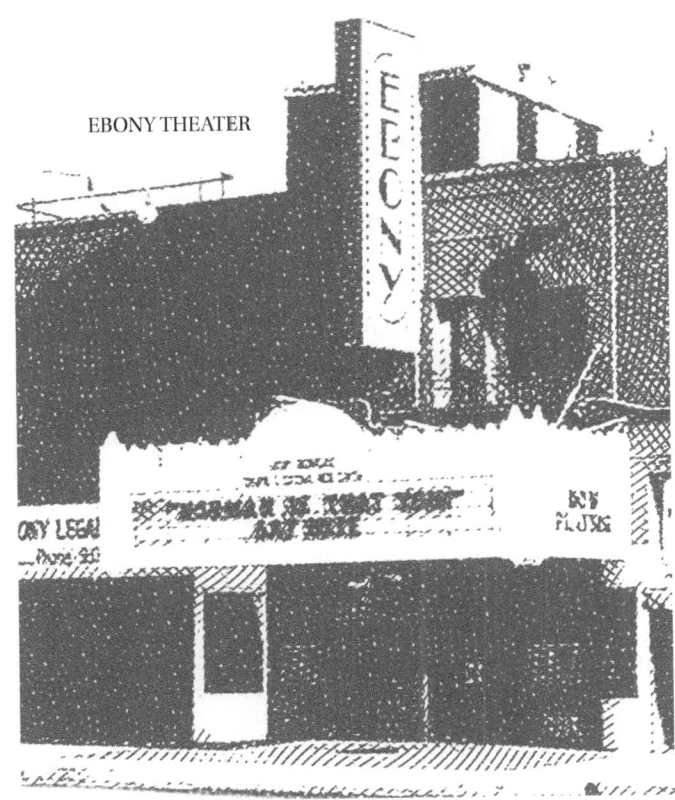

EBONY THEATER

TERESA
GRAVES

NINA MAE
MCKINNEY

ACTRESSES

◼ FIRST BLACK FEMALE MOVIE STAR

Nina Mae McKinney was the first Black actress to achieve success in Hollywood films. McKinney made her debut in 1929 in King Vidor's all-Black musical *Hallelujah!* MGM studios was so impressed by her skills that they signed the then-17-year-old to a long-term contract. McKinney starred in movies like *Safe in Hell* (1931), *Sanders of the River* (1935) and *Gang Smashers* (1938) and is remembered as one of the most dynamic actresses to ever grace the screen. (B. 1912 – D. 1967).

◼ FIRST BLACK ACTRESS TO STAR IN TELEVISION DRAMA SERIES

In the mid-70's Teresa Graves, playing the role of undercover police detective Christie Love in the television (TV) show *Get Christie Love!*, became the first Black actress to star in her own hour–long television crime-drama. Graves began her TV career in the late 1960s as a singer on The Della Reese Show and comedienne on Rowan & Martin's Laugh-In. (B. 1948 – D. 2002).

NINA MAE MCKINNEY
MOVIE FOSTER

■ FIRST BLACK ACADEMY AWARD NOMINEE FOR BEST ACTRESS IN HOLLYWOOD

Dorothy Dandridge broke barriers as one of the first Black actresses to achieve critical acclaim and prominence in mainstream Hollywood films during the 1950s. Born in Ohio in 1922, Dandridge's mother, an entertainer, created a song and dance for her daughters and steered Dorothy and her sister Vivian into show business. Performing as the Wonder Sisters, they traveled the southern United States until 1929's Great Depression ruined business. In 1930, Dandridge's family moved to South LA's Watts/Willowbrook neighborhood where she attended McKinley Junior High School (now George Washington Carver Middle School). Dandridge first appeared onscreen in the mid-1930's in small parts, including *Our Gang comedies* (1935) and Marx brothers movies (1937). She earned her first movie credit in the 1940 film *Four Shall Die*. In 1941, with her appearance in *Chattanooga Choo Choo*, a specialty number in the musical *Sun Valley Serenade*, Dandridge's star really began to shine. In 1951, Dandridge's star began to sizzle. After appearing in the role of Melmendi, Queen of the Ashuba in *Tarzan's Peril* (1951), Dandridge's wardrobe garnered considerable attention and led to her being featured on the cover of *Ebony* magazine (April 1951) and casted *The Harlem Globetrotters* (1951) movie. Dandridge was cast in her first starring role playing opposite of Harry Belafonte in *Bright Road*, a 1953 low-budget film adapted from the Christopher Award-winning short story *See How*

They Run by Mary Elizabeth Vroman. In 1954, Dorothy Dandridge became the first Black woman to receive an Academy Award nomination for Best Actress. Dandridge's portrayal of *Carmen Jones* showcased her acting skills and helped challenge stereotypes surrounding black women in cinema. Throughout her career, Dandridge faced racial discrimination and limited opportunities due to the prevalent racism in Hollywood at the time. Despite these challenges, she persevered and left an enduring legacy as a trailblazer for Black performers. Dandridge died in Hollywood at age 43 in 1965. In 1983, she received a posthumous star on the Hollywood Walk of Fame. (B. 1922 – D. 1965). See *Model* to learn more about Dandridge.

CARMEN JONES MOVIE POSTER

DOROTHY
DANDRIDGE

PAUL R. WILLIAMS

ARCHITECT

■ FIRST BLACK LICENSED ARCHITECT IN CALIFORNIA

Paul R. Williams is one of the most successful and talented architects to ever practice in Los Angeles. In 1920, Williams was appointed to the first Los Angeles City Planning Commission. The following year he became the first certified Black architect in California and the first west of the Mississippi. Known for his versatile and innovative designs, encompassing a wide range of architectural styles, Williams designed over 2,500 homes and commercial buildings and homes, including those of numerous celebrities like Frank Sinatra, Lucille Ball and Desi Arnaz and Lon Chaney. Williams designed a number of landmarks in LA's Black community like First AME Church, 2nd Baptist Church, 28th Street YMCA, the Angelus Funeral Home, and the world-famous LAX theme building. (B. 1894 – D. 1980).

■ FIRST BLACK MEMBER OF AMERICAN INSTITUTE OF ARCHITECTS

In 1923, despite facing racial discrimination and limited opportunities due to his race, Paul R. Williams persevered to become the first Black architect to gain membership in the American Institute of Architects.

■ FIRST BLACK FELLOW AMERICAN INSTITUTE OF ARCHITECTS

In 1957, Paul R. Williams became the first Black person to become an AIA Fellow, the highest honor bestowed by the organization. Williams also served on various architectural boards and advisory councils, advocating for diversity and inclusion in the profession. Williams' architectural legacy extends beyond his buildings. His accomplishments paved the way for future generations of minority architects.

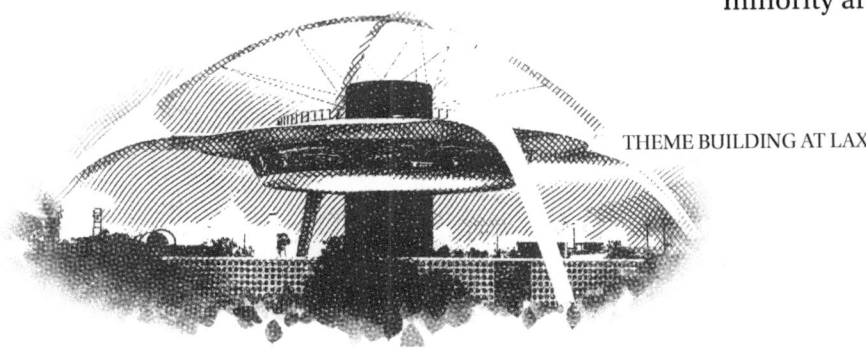

THEME BUILDING AT LAX

BEULAH ECTON WOODARD

ARTISTS

■ FIRST BLACK ARTIST FEATURED IN LOS ANGELES COUNTY MUSEUM OF ART

In 1937, sculptor Beulah Ecton Woodard, an accomplished artist who specialized in African masks, became the first Black artist honored with a solo exhibition at the LA County Museum of Art. Woodard's lifelong interest in African culture began at 12 years old, while attending LA's Polytechnic High, she began to show interest in sculpture and developed her art further with courses at the Los Angeles Art School, the Otis Art Institute, and the University of Southern California. (B. 1895 – D. 1955).

■ FIRST BLACK WOMAN MURALIST IN LOS ANGELES

In the mid-1970s, Alice Patrick's work was recognized by the City of Los Angeles as the first mural painted within the city by a Black woman. However, her original mural was destroyed soon after completion. One of her later works, "Women Do Get Weary But They Don't Give Up" (1991) shows images of Mary McCleod Bethune, Dorothy Height, Oprah Winfrey, Josephine Baker and others. (B. 1948).

BEULAH WOODARD
WORKING

SENGA NENGUDI

EILEEN
ABDULRASHID

ART EXHIBITIONS

■ FIRST BLACK AMERICAN ART EXHIBIT IN LOS ANGELES

The first Black American art exhibition in Los Angeles was hosted in 1929 by the California Art Club in the Hollyhock House at the Barnsdall Art Park in Hollywood. The exhibit was described by local newspapers as consisting of seventy canvases painted by leading Black artists in the United States and included sculpture, etching and photography. The December 1929 issue of the *California Art Club Bulletin* casually mentions that "there will be [Henry Ossawa] Tanner's work among this representative collection. Hanging alongside the highly-decorated Tanner was work by three local artists, Constance Phillips, Paul R. Williams (1894–1980), and A. F. Taynes (Williams and Taynes were also important architects), along with pieces by two other artists from Indiana: John Wesley Hardwick (1891–1968), whose exhibited works included Jesus of Nazareth and landscapes, and organizer William Edouard Scott.

■ FIRST GROUP EXHIBITION OF BLACK WOMEN ARTISTS IN LOS ANGELES

In 1970, Gallery 32, a Black women's art collective founded and run by artist Suzanne Jackson in 1968, hosted "Sapphire Show: You've Come Long Way Baby", the first group exhibition of Black women artists in LA. Gallery 32 was one of the few places in Los Angeles exhibiting the challenging work of emerging Black artists, such as Gloria Bohanon, Suzanne Jackson, Betye Saar, Senga Nengudi, Yvonee Cole Meo, and Eileen Abdulrashid. Jackson said, "Gallery 32 offered a space where people could express an independent voice in their work and not be labeled. Gallery 32 was never a Black gallery, a women's gallery, or a men's gallery; it was a gallery about artists who came through with something to say."

■ FIRST COMPREHENSIVE SURVEY OF BLACK ART BY A MAJOR AMERICAN ART MUSEUM

In 1976, the Los Angeles County Museum of Art (LACMA) opened *Two Centuries of Black American Art* as its major exhibition for the American bicentennial year. It was the first comprehensive survey of Black art which, following its premier at LACMA, toured three other major U.S. art institutions. The premise was to acknowledge the work of Black artists during the period of 1750 to 1950, whose contributions to American art had largely been neglected. Featuring over 200 works and 63 artists, the show included paintings, sculptures, drawing, graphics, crafts and decorative arts.

WILLIAM J. POWELL

AVIATION

■ FIRST BLACK AVIATORS ASSOCIATION IN THE UNITED STATES

In 1928, engineer, soldier, businessman, and aviator William "Bill" J. Powell, along with a number of other visionaries, established the Bessie Coleman Aero Club in Los Angeles, the first ever association of Black aviators in the United States. Powell hoped to inspire Black people to enter aviation not only as pilots, but as designers, engineers and mechanics. He called for them to "fill the air with Black wings". Powell wanted to create opportunities for Blacks in aviation. In his book, *Black Wings*, he wrote, "There is a better job and a better future in aviation for Negroes than in any other industry, and the reason is this: aviation is just beginning its period of growth, and if we get into it now, while it is still uncrowded, we can grow as aviation grows." (B. 1897 – D. 1942).

■ FIRST BLACK FLIGHT SCHOOL IN THE WORLD

In 1930, the Bessie Coleman Aero Club opened the Bessie Coleman Flight School, the world's first all-Black flight school (formerly located at the Los Angeles Eastside Airport).

CURTISS JENNY JN4

31

■ FIRST BLACK-OWNED AIRPLANE MANUFACTURER IN THE UNITED STATES

In the early 1930s William "Bill" J. Powell launched the first Black-owned aircraft manufacturing company, Bessie Coleman Aero, envisioned by Powell as designing and manufacturing aircraft to be flown and serviced by Black people. Unfortunately, as with many businesses, it did not survive the Great Depression.

■ FIRST BLACK AIR SHOW IN LOS ANGELES

On Labor Day in 1931, William "Bill" J. Powell, staged LA's first "All-Black Air Show" at the Los Angeles Eastside Airport.

JAMES BANNING AND THOMAS ALLEN

■ FIRST BLACK PRECISION FLYING TROUPE IN THE UNITED STATES

On Labor Day 1931, a crowd of 15,000 watched the "Five Blackbirds", the nation's first Black precision flying troupe, loop, spin, and dive in formation at LA's Eastside Airport. Although seven Blackbirds actually performed, including one woman, Marie Dickerson, singer and frequent club headliner; it was Hubert Fauntleroy Julian, a pilot known as the crown prince of Black aviation or the "Black Eagle," who garnered all the attention.

■ FIRST BLACK AIRPLANE PILOT TO FLY ACROSS THE UNITED STATES
■ FIRST BLACK AIR NAVIGATOR TO CROSS THE UNITED STATES

On September 19, 1932, motivated by a newspaper promising $1,000 to the first Black pilot to make a coast-to-coast journey, Navigator Thomas Allen and Pilot James Banning set out from LA. They arrived in New York on October 9 making them the first Black pilot and navigator team to fly across the country. Allen (B. 1907 – D. 1989) Banning (B. 1900 – D. 1933).

BESSIE COLEMAN

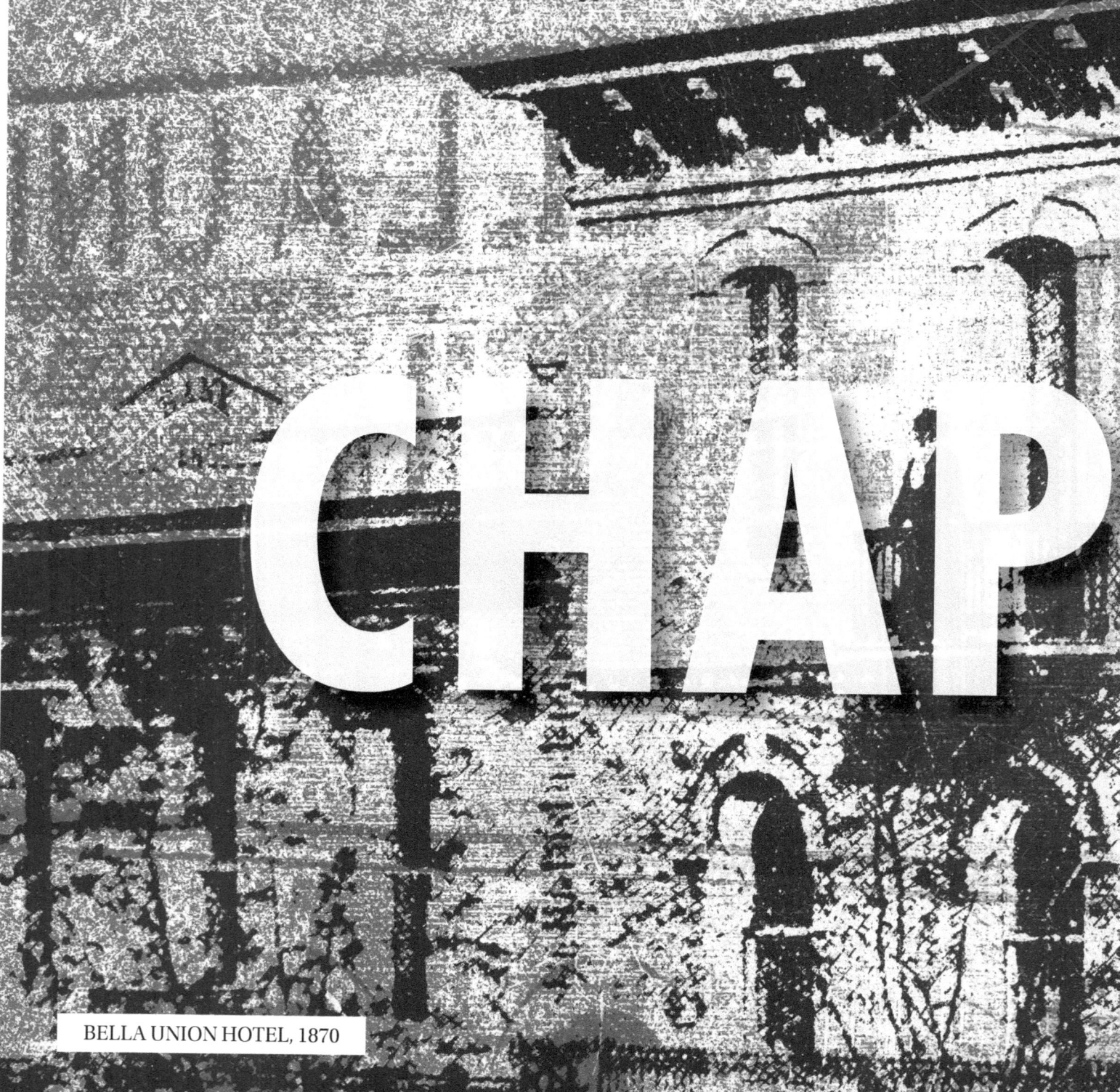

BELLA UNION HOTEL, 1870

ONIE BURNETT
GRANVILLE

BANKER

■ FIRST BLACK-OWNED COMMERCIAL BANK IN CALIFORNIA

Onie Burnett Granville, a visionary real estate broker, founded the Bank of Finance in Los Angeles (LA), the first Black-owned commercial bank in LA. The bank opened its doors on November 16, 1964 at 2651 South Western Avenue. In 1968, Granville opened the Freedom Bank of Finance in Portland, Oregon. Both banks were the first of their kind in their respective cities and among the earliest Black-owned banks in the West. (B. 1916 – D. 1998).

BANK OF FINANCE

BARBERSHOP OWNER

■ FIRST BLACK-OWNED BARBERSHOP IN LOS ANGELES

In the 1850s, Peter Biggs, a former slave, opened LA's first Black-owned barbershop, the New Orleans Shaving Salon, located in the Bella Union Hotel on N. Main Street in present-day downtown LA. In 1865, Biggs, a problematic figure of dubious distinction, became the first Black man arrested for treason in Los Angeles. As reported in the Los Angeles News on April 19, 1865, just five days after Abraham Lincoln's assassination, while much of nation plunged into mourning, and following an order for the arrest of traitors and of persons exulting over the assassination of President Lincoln, "Biggs vociferously proclaimed his ardent attachment to the cause of Secession; whereupon he was promptly arrested and made to foot it, with an iron chain and ball attached to his ankle, all the way from Los Angeles to the U.S. Army Barracks in Wilmington". The reporter noted that, Biggs gave three cheers for the Confederacy when meeting acquaintances along the road. (B. Unknown – D. 1869). See *Head of Household* to learn more about Biggs.

LARRY FARMER

CHERYL MILLER

BASKETBALL COACHES

FIRST BLACK MEN'S HEAD BASKETBALL COACH AT THE UNIVERSITY OF CALIFORNIA LOS ANGELES (UCLA)

In 1981, at the age of 30, Larry Farmer made his debut as UCLA's first Black Men's Head Basketball Coach. As an athlete, Farmer finished his Bruin career in 1973 with the best win-loss tally of any National College Athletic Association (NCAA) player in history, participating in all the games for the UCLA teams that went 89–1 (.989), the best winning percentage in NCAA men's basketball history. (B. 1951).

FIRST BLACK MEN'S HEAD BASKETBALL COACH AT UNIVERSITY OF SOUTHERN CALIFORNIA (USC)

George Raveling, USC's first Black Men's Head Basketball Coach, was at the university from 1986 to 1994, taking the Trojans to two NCAA tournament appearances and earning national Coach of the Year recognition in 1992 and 1994. Raveling was elected into the Naismith Basketball Hall of Fame in February 2015. (B. 1937).

FIRST BLACK WOMEN'S HEAD BASKETBALL COACH AT THE UNIVERSITY OF SOUTHERN CALIFORNIA (USC)

In 1993, Cheryl Miller, USC's career scoring and rebounding leader, was offered the coaching job of the women's basketball team, making her USC's first Black women's basketball head coach. (B. 1964).

FIRST BLACK FEMALE BASKETBALL COACH FOR THE LOS ANGELES LAKERS

In 2021, Eshaya "Shay" Murphy, a Southern California native who played her college ball at USC, became the first woman hired as an assistant coach by the Lakers. (B. 1985).

VINTAGE BASKETBALL

DON BARKSDALE

BASKETBALL STAR

■ FIRST BLACK COLLEGE BASKETBALL ALL-AMERICAN IN LOS ANGELES

In 1947, Don Barksdale became the first Black person to be named to the Helms Foundation All-America team after helping the UCLA Bruins to the Pacific Coast Conference championship. The following year, Barksdale represented the United States in basketball at the London Olympics, becoming the first Black person to make the U.S. Olympic basketball team and the first to win gold. In 1953, Barksdale was the first Black player to be named to the NBA All-Star game. A documentary on Barksdale's life, *Bounce: The Don Barksdale Story*, was released in 2007. (B. 1923 – D. 1993).

DON BARKSDALE
IN ACTION

BEAUTY SCHOOL FOUNDER

■ FIRST BLACK COSMETOLOGY SCHOOL WEST OF THE MISSISSIPPI

In 1930, an era when Blacks found the cosmetology field closed to them because there was no place for training, Hazel Dell Williams and Henrietta Kent opened the Henrietta Beauty School at 18th Street and Central Avenue in Los Angeles, the first cosmetology school for Blacks west of the Mississippi River. The school, now operating as the Universal College of Beauty in South Central Los Angeles has sent thousands of licensed graduates into the field. Williams also founded the California Cosmetology Legislative Education Committee, a lobbying organization in Sacramento for Black beauticians. The school is currently owned by her grandson, Kenneth Williams, and run by her great-granddaughter, Jasmine Williams.

41

DR. CHARLES R. DREW

BLOOD BANK

■ FIRST INTERRACIAL BLOOD BANK IN LOS ANGELES

In 1942, the Red Cross established the first interracial blood bank at Rose-Netta Hospital in the city of Los Angeles. Here's the backstory. In February of 1941, the Red Cross began the National Blood Donor Service to collect blood for the U.S. military with Dr. Charles R. Drew, as medical director. Initially, the Red Cross announced that while it would accept blood from Black donors, it would segregate it. In early 1942, in objection to this discriminatory medical practice policy, Drew resigned from the Red Cross position, stating that there was no scientific evidence of any difference between the blood of people from different races, and that the policy was insulting to Black people. In 1944, Drew noted that "it is fundamentally wrong for any great nation to willfully discriminate against such a large group of its people. One can say quite truthfully that on the battlefields nobody is very interested in where the plasma comes from when they are hurt."

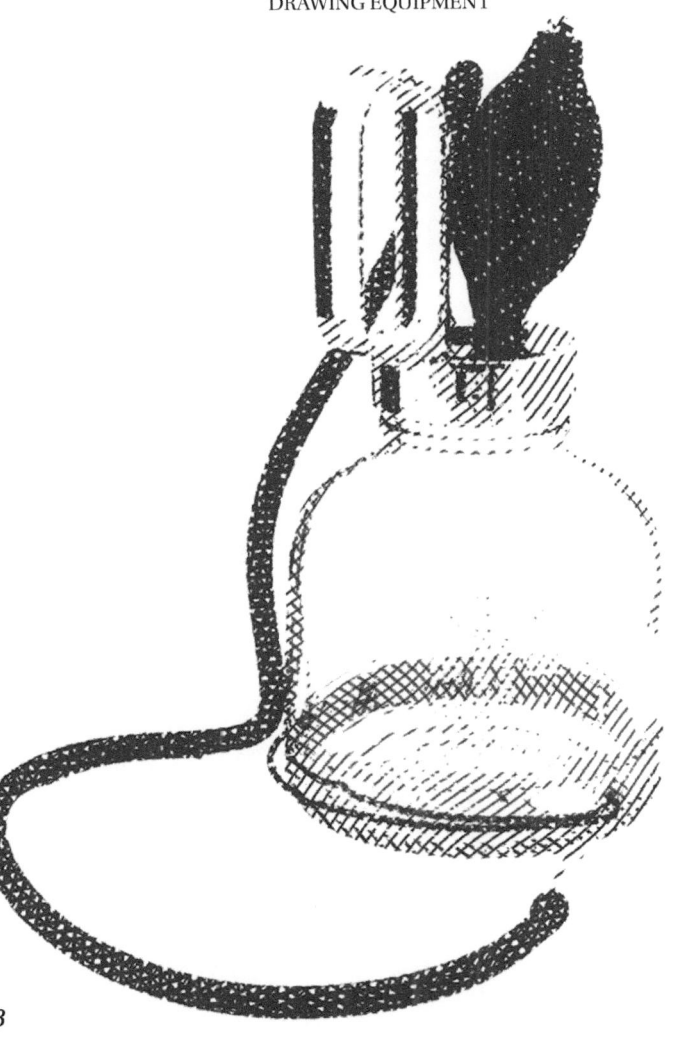

VINTAGE BLOOD
DRAWING EQUIPMENT

MARK RIDLEY-THOMAS

BOARD OF SUPERVISORS MEMBERS

■ FIRST BLACK PERSON APPOINTED TO LOS ANGELES COUNTY BOARD OF SUPERVISORS (LACBOS)
■ FIRST BLACK PERSON ELECTED TO LACBOS

In 1979, then Governor Jerry Brown appointed Yvonne Brathwaite Burke to fill a vacancy on the LACBOS making her both LA's first female and first Black county supervisor. She served one term. Years later, Burke's 1992 LACBOS election victory made her the first Black person elected to the board. Burke served as LACBOS Chair three times (1993–94, 1997–98, 2002–03) and finished her final term in 2008. (B. 1932). See *Congressional Representatives from Los Angeles* to learn more about Burke.

■ FIRST POLITICIAN OF ANY RACE/ ETHNICITY ELECTED TO CALIFORNIA STATE ASSEMBLY, CALIFORNIA SENATE, LA CITY COUNCIL & THE LA COUNTY BOARD OF SUPERVISORS

In winning the 2008 LACBOS election, Mark Ridley-Thomas became the first person of any race, ethnicity or gender to serve in the California Assembly (2002–2006), California Senate (2006–2008), LA City Council (1991–2002 and 2020–2022) and the LACBOS (2008–2020). In 2021, after more than two decades of public service, Ridley-Thomas was indicted on federal corruption charges and, in 2023, convicted of bribery, conspiracy, honest services mail fraud and honest services wire fraud. On 8/28/2023, a U.S. District Court judge sentenced Ridley-Thomas to 3.5 years imprisonment, 3 years supervised release, and a $30,000 fine. Note: at the time of publication, the case was under appeal. (B. 1954).

KENNETH HAHN
HALL OF ADMINISTRATION

ARCOLA
PHILPOTT

BUS DRIVER

■ FIRST BLACK BUS OPERATOR IN LOS ANGELES

The Los Angeles Railway company (LARY) was not previously known as a socially progressive organization, nor were many other industries or job markets of the early 1940s. However, in August of 1944, and without much fanfare, LARY hired its first Black bus operator, Mrs. Arcola Philpott. Referred to as a "motormanette", Philpott worked out of Arthur Winston Division 5 and drove the "F" line from 116th/South Vermont Avenue to Union Station, traveling up Vermont to Santa Barbara (now Martin Luther King Boulevard), Grand, Jefferson, Main, Macy (now Cesar Chavez Blvd) to the Union Station Passenger Terminal.

Within a few weeks of hiring Mrs. Philpott, Los Angeles Railway also hired its first Black motorman. The Los Angeles Sentinel and the California Eagle, LA's leading Black newspapers took notice, observing that the racial integration of the ranks of bus and train operators was a major change from past practices, skillfully negotiated by the Reverend Clayton Russell's Los Angeles Negro Victory Comittee, the AFL-CIO, the NAACP, the Fair Employment Practices Commission and the reform-minded Los Angeles Mayor Fletcher Bowron. (B. Unknown – D. 1991).

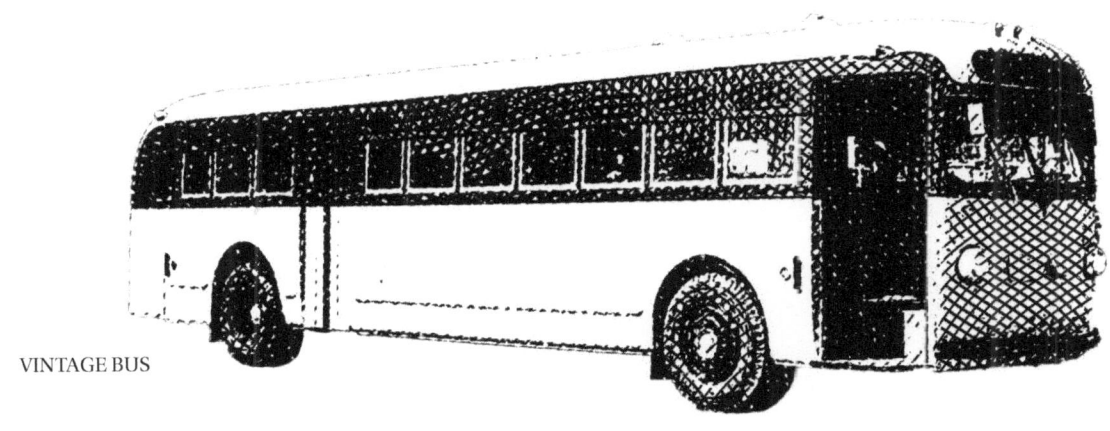

VINTAGE BUS

47

ROBERT
CURRY OWENS

BUSINESS OWNERS

■ FIRST BLACK-OWNED COMMERCIAL BUSINESS BUILDING IN LOS ANGELES

In the early 1890s, Robert Curry Owens constructed a two-story brick structure on Broadway, the first Black-owned commercial business building in downtown Los Angeles (LA). In 1905, Owens constructed a six-story building in downtown Los Angeles worth $250,000, which for many years was the largest Black-owned structure west of the Mississippi River. Owens, a native-born Angeleno, was the son of Charles Owens, owner of The Owens Livery Stable, and the grandson of Biddy Mason, LA's first Black million-aire. As the first born heir to the Owens-Mason family fortune, Owens was once the wealthiest Black man in LA and, for many decades, one of the most powerful in California. (B. 1860 – D. 1929.est).

■ FIRST BLACK-OWNED FUNERAL HOME IN LOS ANGELES

In 1905, the Porter-Roberts Company, a joint venture between Andrew J. Roberts and William Porter, opened the first Black-owned funeral home in Los Angeles. The business was located at 12th and San Pedro Streets (building has been demolished).

■ FIRST BLACK-OWNED BUSINESS INCORPORATED IN CALIFORNIA

In 1925, the Angelus Funeral Home became the first Black-owned business incorporated in California. The original building, located at 1030 Jefferson Blvd., is recognized as number 774 on the list of Los Angeles Historic-Cultural Monuments. Their current building, located at 3875 S. Crenshaw Blvd., was the first Black-owned property on the "Shaw".

A. J. ROBERTS SON & CO
FUNERAL HOME

CITY HALL, LOS ANGELES, 1935

FREDERICK
MADISON ROBERTS

CALIFORNIA STATE POLITICAL REPRESENTATIVES FROM LA

■ FIRST BLACK PERSON ELECTED TO THE CALIFORNIA STATE ASSEMBLY

On January 6, 1919, Frederick Madison Roberts, a politician, journalist and newspaper owner, became the first Black person to serve in the California State Assembly. His district included south Los Angeles (LA) and surrounding cities. Roberts sponsored anti-lynching bills; measures to improve public education; legislation addressing civil rights; and, a bill to establish the University of California at Los Angeles. In June of 1922, he welcomed Marcus Garvey, the founder of the Universal Negro Improvement Association, to LA and rode in his parade car. He served in the assembly for 16 years, representing LA until 1934. His father, Andrew J. Roberts, was proprietor of LA's first Black-owned funeral home. (B. 1919 – D. 1952).

■ FIRST BLACK CALIFORNIA STATE SENATOR

In 1966, Mervyn Dymally, a Los Angeles teacher and politician, became the first Black person to serve in the California State Senate. (B. 1926 – D. 2012). See *Governor/Lt. Governor* to learn more Dymally.

■ FIRST BLACK PERSON FROM TRINIDAD ELECTED TO CALIFORNIA STATE ASSEMBLY

In 1962, Mervyn Dymally became the first Black person elected to serve in the California State Assembly who was not born in the United States. After emigrating from Trinidad at age 19, Dymally graduated from Cal State LA and became a public school teacher. After that, Dymally served in the California State Assembly (1963–1966 and 2002–2008), the State Senate (1967–1975), Lt. Governor (1975–1979) and twelve years as a congressman in the U.S. House of Representatives (1981–1993).

■ FIRST BLACK WOMAN ELECTED SPEAKER OF CALIFORNIA STATE LEGISLATURE

In 2008, Karen Bass was elected to serve as the 67th Speaker of the California State Assembly, making her the first Black woman in U.S. history to serve as the Speaker of a state-wide legislative body. (B. 1953). See *Mayors* to learn more about Bass.

GRANT D. VENERABLE

JAMES E. LUVALLE

CHEMISTS

▮ FIRST BLACK GRADUATE OF CALIFORNIA INSTITUTE OF TECHNOLOGY (CALTECH)

In 1932, Grant D. Venerable became the first Black graduate of the California Institute of Technology, earning a BS in Chemistry. During his time at Caltech Venerable served as the president of the Caltech Cosmopolitan Club, an organization that was formed to promote fellowship among diverse nationalities, contributed to the student newspaper, and participated in athletics. In 2021, an undergraduate residence hall at Caltech, the Grant D. Venerable House, was renamed in his honor. (B. 1904 – D. 1986).

VINTAGE BEAKERS

▮ FIRST BLACK DOCTORAL GRADUATE OF CALIFORNIA INSTITUTE OF TECHNOLOGY (CALTECH)

Prior to earning his doctorate in chemistry and mathematics at Caltech, James E. LuValle, the world's fastest chemist, was a track star at the University of California Los Angeles (UCLA) and won the bronze medal in the 400-meter dash at the historic 1936 Olympics in Berlin, Germany. Despite his athletic prowess, LuValle didn't have an athletic scholarship, because UCLA did not award track scholarships back then, he paid his way through college with an academic scholarship and a job in one of UCLA's chemistry labs.

In 1936, after achieving a straight-A average, UCLA awarded LuValle a bachelor degree in chemistry. In 1937, the same institution awarded him a master's degree in chemistry and physics. In 1940, after completing his doctoral research studies under the tutelage of the renowned chemist, Dr. Linus Pauling, James E. LuValle became the the first Black person to earn a Ph.D. from Caltech. (B. 1912 – D. 1993).

ERNEST
MORRISON

ALLEN
HOSKINS

CHILD ACTORS

■ FIRST BLACK CHILDREN IN MOVIE ACTING ENSEMBLE IN HOLLYWOOD

In the 1920's Hollywood film producer Hal Roach's *Our Gang/Little Rascals* actors ensemble included several Black children like Ernest "Sunshine Sammy" Morrison (the first Black child movie star in Hollywood) and Allen Hoskins, who was just one year old when he began. Hoskins, who played the character named Farina, remained with the ensemble through the silent picture years and the transition to talking motion pictures, eventually leaving the series at the age of eleven. From 1930 to 1935, Matthew Beard Jr. was one of the most well-known member of the troupe. He was famous for portraying the character of Stymie, a self-assured and nonchalant kid who was always ready with a set of clever ideas to solve any of the problems he might face. Although Stymie was the best-known, Buckwheat is one of the most remembered *Our Gang/Little Rascals* characters. Portrayed by William Billie Thomas Jr., Buckwheat first appeared in 1935. Thomas Jr. is immortalized in cinema for coining Buckwheat's unforgettable catchphrase "O-tay". Thomas Jr. stayed with the series until it ended in 1944. Morrison (B. 1912 – D. 1989). Hoskins (B. 1920 – D.1980). Beard Jr. (B. 1925 – D. 1981). Thomas Jr. (B. 1931 – D.1980).

■ FIRST BLACK CHILD MOVIE STAR IN HOLLYWOOD

In 1919, after observing little Ernest Frederick Morrison's acting ability, movie producer Hal Roach of *Our Gang/Little Rascals* fame signed him to a contract and created *The Sunshine Sammy* comedy series. Roach paid Morrison $10,000 a year, making him both the first Black child signed to a long-term contract and the highest paid child actor in Hollywood at the time. When Roach conceived the *Our Gang/ Little Rascals* motion picture series, Morrison was one of the first children recruited. Morrison retired from film in the 1940s. In 1987, after appearing in over 145 motion pictures including the *East Side Kids* series, Morrison was inducted into the Black Filmmakers Hall of Fame. (B. 1912 – D. 1989).

THE BUCCANEERS POSTER

CARL BEAN

CHURCHES

FIRST BLACK CHURCH IN LOS ANGELES

In 1872, Biddy Mason's the Curry-Owens family and others helped found the First African Methodist Episcopal (FAME) Church, the oldest church founded by Black people in the city of Los Angeles. Mason, who arrived in California in 1851 as a captive slave, won a landmark court case in 1856 to gain freedom for herself and her daughters and thirteen others, used the money she had earned as a nurse and midwife to invest in commercial real estate and amassed a sizeable fortune. When the church formed, initially the members gathered in Mason's home. In 1888, sixteen years later, Mason helped finance the purchase of a church building on Azusa Street.

FIRST LGBTQ+ AFFIRMING AND WELCOMING BLACK CHURCH

In 1982, Archbishop Carl Bean, a former Motown musician, founded the Unity Fellowship Church, America's first Lesbian, Gay, Bisexual, Transgender, & Queer (LGBTQ) affirming and welcoming Black church, in South Los Angeles (LA). In 1985, Bean founded the Minority AIDS Project, also in South LA, to address the needs of individuals within Black and Latino communities who were living with HIV/AIDS. MAP provides prevention, care and treatment services for people who need them. (B. 1944 – D. 2021).

FISRT AME CHURCH

DOUGLAS
DOLLARHIDE

GILBERT
W. LINDSAY

CITY COUNCIL MEMBERS

■ FIRST BLACK PERSON ON THE LOS ANGELES CITY COUNCIL

In 1963, at the age of 62, and after working decades for the city as a janitor, Gilbert W. Lindsay was appointed to a vacant 9th District Council seat, making him the first Black officeholder in Los Angeles (LA) since the Spanish period. Later that year, he won the election and, over his career, was reelected to eight successive terms. The gravel-voiced councilman, although only 5 feet, 3 inches tall, was a giant among politicians in LA. As the self-proclaimed "Emperor of the Great 9th," Lindsay regarded the rejuvenation of the downtown area of his district as his greatest accomplishment. Upon his death in 1990, then LA Mayor Tom Bradley said Councilman Lindsay was a dynamic force whose appointment to the City Council in January of 1963 opened the doors of political power to all residents with his district. (B. 1900 – D. 1990).

■ FIRST BLACK PEOPLE ELECTED TO LOS ANGELES CITY COUNCIL

In winning their respective 1963 Los Angeles City Council District elections, Billy G. Mills (8th district), Gilbert W. Lindsey (9th district) and Tom Bradley (10th district) became the first three Black people ever elected, and reelected in 1967 and 1971, to the council.

After the '63 election, Mills noted that the "cheek has turned and now Caucasians will realize that you don't have to be white to represent whites." Mills (B. 1929). Bradley (B. 1917. – D. 1993).

■ FIRST BLACK PERSON ELECTED TO COMPTON CITY COUNCIL

In 1963, Douglas Dollarhide, formerly a postal worker, was elected Compton's first Black City Council member. Dollarhide won his council district's election by just 75 votes. During his three terms on the council, Dollarhide served on the finance committee and represented the city at the League of California Cities. In June of 1969, Dollarhide became the first Black person to be elected mayor of Compton. (B. 1923 – D. 2008).

■ FIRST BLACK WOMAN ON LOS ANGELES CITY COUNCIL

On June 6, 1991, Rita Walters was elected to office making her the first Black woman to serve on the LA City Council. Walters said "my largest energies will be focused on upgrading services to the district, and that her first priority would be to clean the place up." Walters served on the council from 1991 through 2001. (B. 1930 – D. 2020).

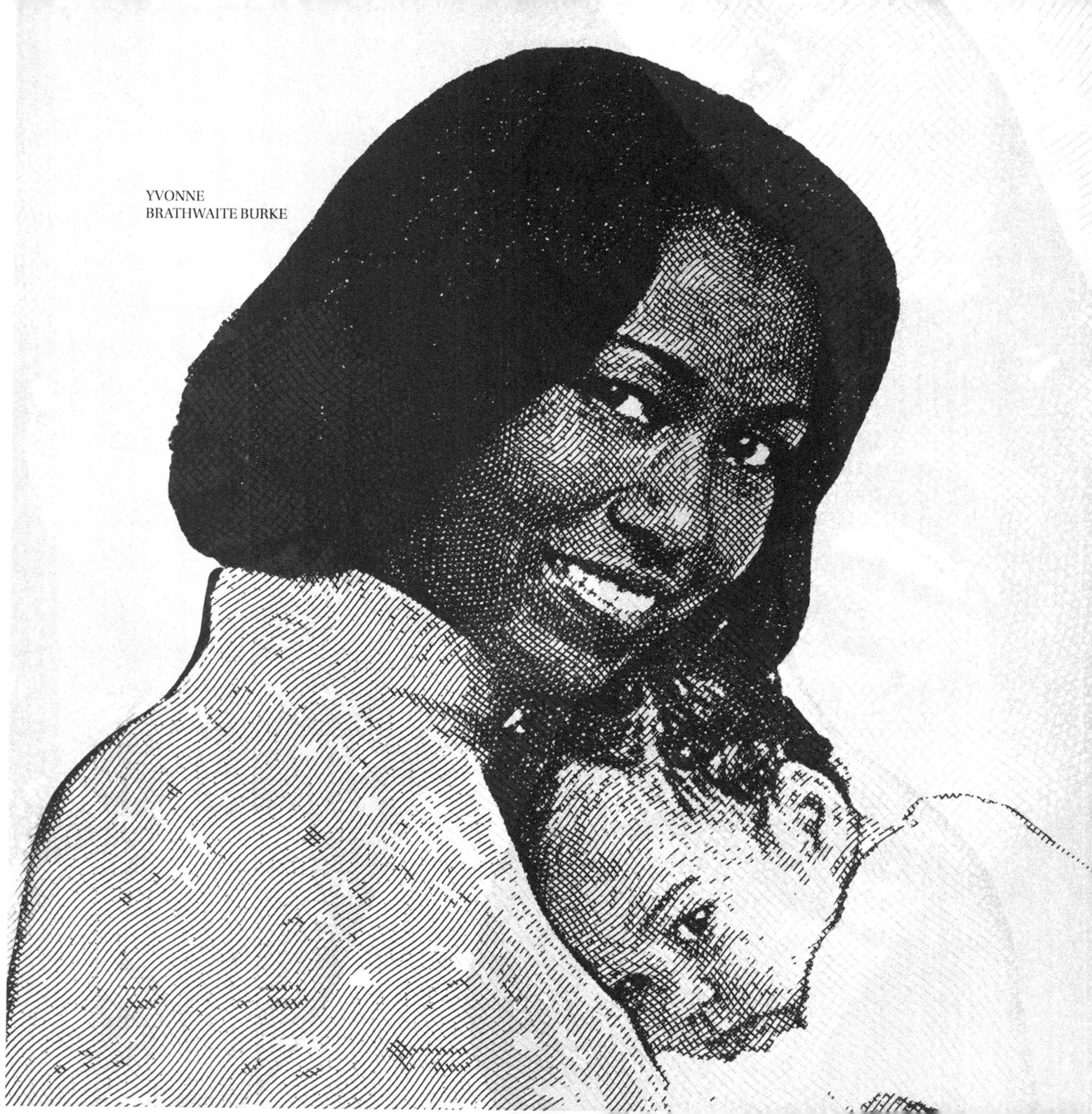

YVONNE
BRATHWAITE BURKE

CONGRESSIONAL REPRESENTATIVES FROM LOS ANGELES

■ FIRST BLACK PERSON ELECTED TO CONGRESS FROM CALIFORNIA

With his 1963 election victory, Augustus F. Hawkins became the first Black person from California, and the first Black congressional representative from west of the Mississippi River to serve in the U.S. Congress. Augustus F. Hawkins began his political career in the California State Assembly where he served from 1935 through 1963. A Black person of mixed-race ancestry, Hawkins' was very fair-skinned. Throughout his life, he was often assumed to be of solely white ancestry, however, he refused to pass as white. Hawkins political career spanned 56 years of public service in the California Assembly (28 years) and the U.S. House of Representatives (28 years). (B. 1907 – D. 2007).

■ FIRST BLACK WOMAN ELECTED TO CONGRESS FROM CALIFORNIA

In 1973, Yvonne Brathwaite Burke became the first female and first Black woman to represent the West Coast in the US Congress where she represented the 93rd Congressional District until 1979. While there, Burke became the first United States Congressperson to give birth during her political term. (B. 1932).

AUGUSTUS F. HAWKINS

WALLACE "WALLY" AMOS

ODEY C. UKPO

COOKIE KING

▌ FIRST BLACK COOKIE KING

In the mid-1970's, long before Mrs. Fields and the legion of cookie shops that now tempt us, Wallace "Wally" Amos became the proud owner of the Famous Amos Chocolate Chip Cookie Store, perhaps the first cookie-centric store in the United States. Best known as "Famous Amos", Amos expertly combined self-promotion, salesmanship and baking abilities to create a cookie empire. His first store opened on March 10, 1975, as a small, father-and-son operation. His son Shawn said back then "when the store first opened, he and I were together. It was him in the back making cookies and me standing on a milk crate in the front, selling them." Today, an LA city historical marker sits in front of 7181 Sunset Blvd. designating the block as Famous Amos Square and commemorating America's first "cookie" store. (B. 1936). See *Talent Agent* for more information about Amos.

CORONER

▌ FIRST BLACK LOS ANGELES COUNTY CORONER

On November 4, 2022, Dr. Odey C. Ukpo became the first Black person to serve as Los Angeles County coroner since the office was established in 1850. The coroner investigates and determines the circumstances, manner and cause of all violent, sudden or unusual deaths occurring within LA County, including the city of Los Angeles, 87 other municipalities and its unincorporated areas. (B. circa 1979).

LA COUNTY CORONER'S BUILDING

CHAP

USC SCHOOL OF DENTISTRY, 1898

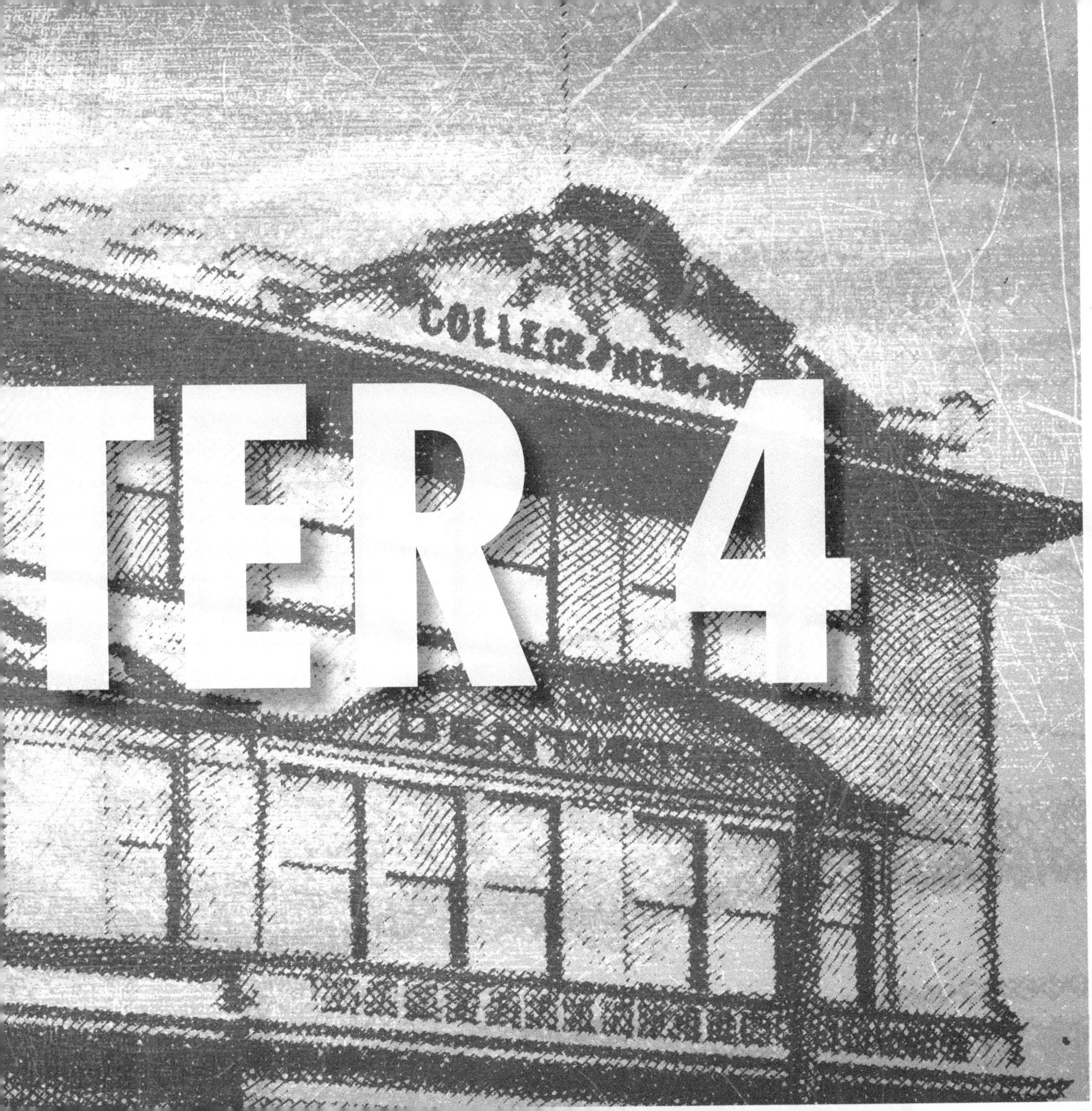
TER 4
COLLEGE

VADA AND JOHN
SOMERVILLE

DENTAL SCHOOL GRADUATES

■ FIRST BLACK FEMALE GRADUATE FROM UCLA SCHOOL OF DENTISTRY

In 1974, Dr. Linda Lott became the first Black female to graduate from the UCLA School of Dentistry. (B. Unknown).

■ FIRST BLACK MALE GRADUATE OF UNIVERSITY OF SOUTHERN CALIFORNIA DENTAL SCHOOL

In 1903, John Alexander Somerville became the first Black person to enter, and later graduate (in 1907) from, the School of Dentistry at USC. Responding to Jim-Crow era laws and segregation, Somerville said, "I made a resolution that I would work at any job that I could find, no matter how menial, until I saved enough money to enter an institution of higher learning to prepare myself for a trade or profession. I wanted to earn a place where I would not have to ask any other fellow for a job." (B. 1881 – D. 1973). See *Police Overseers* for more information on Somerville.

■ FIRST BLACK WOMAN DOCTOR OF DENTISTRY AT UNIVERSITY OF SOUTHERN CALIFORNIA DENTAL SCHOOL

In 1918, Vada Watson Somerville became the first Black woman to become a Doctor of Dentistry at USC and the second Black woman to receive a Doctor of Dental Surgery degree in the state of California. Somerville was married to John Somerville, USC's first Black dental school graduate. (B. 1885 – D. 1972). See *Dentists* for information on Watson Somerville.

USC SCHOOL OF DENTISTRY

ALVA CURTIS GARROTT

DENTISTS

▪ FIRST BLACK LICENSED DENTIST IN LOS ANGELES

Dr. Alva Curtis Garrott earned degrees in Pharmacy and Dentistry at Howard University in Washington, D. C. before bringing his family to Los Angeles. In 1901, Dr. Garrott opened an office in the Wilson Block at the corner of 1st and Spring Street (building has been demolished) making him the first Black licensed dentist in Los Angeles. In 1907, his wife, Lillie De Jarnette Garrott, was suffering from a medical condition and the family moved from Los Angeles into temporary housing in Glendale. Several months after their arrival, they received a threatening letter that opened, "to the only colored man in Glendale" warning the family that they would suffer consequences if they did not move immediately. Terrorized but without options, the family stayed in Glendale until Lillie died in 1916. (B. 1866 – D. 1952).

▪ FIRST BLACK WOMAN LICENSED TO PRACTICE DENTISTRY IN CALIFORNIA

Prior to becoming a dentist, Vada Watson was a telephone operator and bookkeeper when, in 1912, she married John Somerville, a dentist. With his encouragement, Watson-Somerville applied to dental school and, in 1918, she became the first Black woman to graduate from the University of Southern California School of Dentistry and the first Black woman to be licensed to practice dentistry in the state of California. In 1933, after ten years in practice together, Watson-Somerville retired from dentistry to focus on community activism (e.g. founding the Los Angeles branch of the National Association for the Advancement of Colored People) and entrepreneurism (e.g. building the Hotel Somerville/Dunbar Hotel). (B. 1885 – D. 1972). See *Dental School Graduates* for more information about Somerville.

VINTAGE MOUTH MIRROR

MARION L. OBERA

CONSUELO
BLAND MARSHALL

DISTRICT ATTORNEYS

■ FIRST BLACK DEPUTY DISTRICT ATTORNEY IN LOS ANGELES

In 1930, Leon Whitaker became the first Black Deputy District Attorney west of Chicago. Whitaker died the following year during an appendix operation. (B. 1904 – D. 1931).

■ FIRST BLACK FEMALE DEPUTY CITY ATTORNEY IN LOS ANGELES

In 1962, Consuelo Bland Marshall became the first Black woman to work in the LA City Attorney's office. Bland served from 1962 to 1967. (B. 1936).

■ FIRST BLACK FEMALE DEPUTY DISTRICT ATTORNEY IN LOS ANGELES

In 1963, Marion L. Obera was appointed Deputy District Attorney of Los Angeles County. Obera graduated from University of California Los Angeles in 1956 with a degree in pre-social welfare and, in 1962, she earned her law degree from the University of Southern California Law School. Obera, who was known as "Maximum Marion" for her tough approach to sentencing, received an annual salary of $29,270. (B. Unknown).

■ FIRST BLACK ASSISTANT DISTRICT ATTORNEY IN LOS ANGELES COUNTY

In 1978, Johnnie Cochran became the first Black male Assistant District Attorney in Los Angeles County. Cochran's is best known for his classic line from the 1995 OJ case "If it don't fit, you must acquit" which won the acquittal and was probably the coolest legal line uttered in the last century. (B. 1937 – D. 2005).

JOHNNIE L. COCHRAN

■ FIRST BLACK LOS ANGELES COUNTY DISTRICT ATTORNEY

In winning the 2012 election, Jackie Lacey became the first Black person to serve as District Attorney of Los Angeles County. Lacey said she "...grew up in a working-class home in the Crenshaw district of South Los Angeles and attended Dorsey High School. Lacey said..." my community shaped me in every way and led me to pursue a career as a prosecutor. I witnessed vulnerable people in my community who did not have access or knowledge of the justice system.

I was drawn to public service because I wanted to be a voice for those people. I wanted to make a difference for people like my father who was shot and never received justice. I also wanted to reform areas of our criminal justice system that are not fair and perpetuate inequality. These values still drive me every day."

LA CIVIC CENTER

JACKIE LACEY

LEONARD
STOVALL

MONROE ALPHEUS
MAJORS

DOCTORS

▪ FIRST BLACK PERSON TO PASS THE CALIFORNIA BOARD OF MEDICAL EXAMINATION
▪ FIRST BLACK MEDICAL DOCTOR IN LOS ANGELES

In 1888, Dr. Monroe Alpheus Majors, a graduate of Meharry Medical College in Nashville (1886), became the first Black person to pass the California Board of Medical Examination and earn a medical license in California, where he practiced in Los Angeles from 1888 to 1890. Majors left the state in 1890, returning to Los Angeles in 1933 where he died aged 96 in 1960.

▪ FIRST BLACK WOMAN MEDICAL DOCTOR IN THE STATE OF CALIFORNIA
▪ FIRST BLACK WOMAN MEDICAL DOCTOR IN LOS ANGELES

In 1918, Ruth Janetta Temple, the first Black woman to graduate from Loma Linda University with a bachelor's degree in medicine, became the first Black female licensed to practice medicine in California. Temple worked to create public health services for LA's underserved low-income communities. The Dr. Ruth Temple Health Care Center located at 3834 S. Western Ave., LA 90062 is named in her honor.

▪ FIRST BLACK MEDICAL DOCTOR AT LOS ANGELES COUNTY GENERAL HOSPITAL

In 1930, Dr. Leonard Stovall, upon his appointment to the tuberculosis section of the staff of the Los Angeles City General Hospital, became LA County's first Black medical doctor on staff. In 1933, realizing the need for health education, and recognizing that there were practically no hospitals in Los Angeles that would admit and treat Black people for tuberculosis, Stovall established a 50-bed hospital for patients of all races suffering from tuberculosis.

▪ FIRST BLACK DOCTOR HIRED BY KAISER HEALTH GROUP IN LOS ANGELES

In 1954, Kaiser Harbor City's Medical Director hired Dr. Raleigh Bledsoe making him the first Black physician on Kaiser's Southern California medical staff. A native of Texas, Bledsoe attended Compton College and the University of California, Los Angeles. While serving in the Army, Bledsoe earned his medical degree from Meharry Medical College in Tennessee. After interning at Los Angeles County General Hospital, Bledsoe served as a captain in the U.S. Army Medical Corps from 1945-48 and was a member of the Tuskegee Airmen. He later completed his residency in radiology at the University of Southern California.

CHAP

LOS ANGELES BOARD OF PUBLIC WORKS HEARING ROOM, 1928

TER. 5

LOIS COOPER

ENGINEERS

▮ FIRST BLACK ENGINEER AT JET PROPULSION LABORATORY (JPL)

In 1952, after earning a bachelor's degree in chemical engineering at the University of California Los Angeles, Janez Lawson became the first Black engineer hired by JPL. (B. 1930 – D. 1990).

▮ FIRST BLACK ENGINEER AT CAL STATE LONG BEACH (CSULB)

In 1967, Jeffrey Clements became the first Black person to earn a degree from the Mechanical & Aerospace Engineering Department at CSULB. (B. Unknown).

▮ FIRST BLACK TRANSPORTATION ENGINEER IN CALIFORNIA

In 1953, Lois Cooper became the first Black female engineer hired by the California Department of Transportation (Caltrans). Upon her hire, Cooper said 'even though Caltrans may not have wanted a woman, let alone a Black woman, here I am calculating all these freeway alignments'. Cooper worked on the Century Freeway project, now the '105', and was the first female director of the Diamond Lane project, a precursor to carpool lanes. (B. 1931 – D. 2014).

JANEZ LAWSON AND THE THE WOMEN OF THE JET PROPULSION LABORATORY

FESIA DAVENPORT

ERICA BLYTHER

ENVIRONMENTAL HEALTH ADMIN

EXECUTIVE OFFICER

▌ FIRST BLACK WOMAN TO HEAD OFFICE OF PETROLEUM AND NATURAL GAS ADMINISTRATION AND SAFETY

In June 2021, the Los Angeles Board of Public Works appointed environmental scientist Erica Blyther to the position of Petroleum Administrator for the Office of Petroleum and Natural Gas Administration and Safety. Blyther said "oil and gas issues in Los Angeles are incredibly complex, and managing them requires a deep understanding of the issues our communities face, strong relationships with our partners and local leaders, and solutions to make LA less reliant on drilling and fossil fuels." (B. Unknown).

▌ FIRST BLACK CHIEF EXECUTIVE OFFICER FOR LOS ANGELES COUNTY

In January 2021, Fesia Davenport was appointed Chief Executive Officer (CEO) of Los Angeles County. As CEO, Davenport is responsible for a $38.2 billion budget, operationalizing policy initiatives, coordinating strategic communication, managing capital projects and administering policies and regulations. (B. Unknown).

LA OIL FIELDS

LOS ANGELES FIRE DEPARTMENT, MAIN ST., 1871

JOHN SINGLETON

FILM DIRECTOR

∎ FIRST BLACK ACADEMY AWARD NOMINEE FOR BEST DIRECTOR

John Singleton graduated from the John Wells Division of Writing for Screen & Television at the USC School of Cinematic Arts in 1990. While at USC, he won the Jack Nicholson Screenwriting Award two years in a row: in 1988 for Twilight Time, then in 1989 for Boyz n the Hood, a coming-of-age crime drama about three childhood friends growing up in the crime-ridden neighborhood of South Central LA, which he wrote as his senior thesis on a campus library computer. Boyz n the Hood made its Los Angeles premier on July 2, 1991 and was a smash hit. However, although not directly linked to the movie, the opening was accompanied by violence. According to the LA Times, "When Boyz N the Hood opened, at least 11 people were wounded from gunfire at Southern California theaters. At least 25 violent incidents were reported at theaters nationwide". In February of 1992, Boyz in the Hood led to Singleton being nominated for the Best Director Award by the Academy of Motion Picture Arts and Sciences and making him, at age 24, both the youngest and first Black person to be so nominated.

The film also received a nomination for the Best Original Screenplay award. Despite Boyz in the Hood's popularity, many consider Singleton's Poetic Justice (1993), featuring Janet Jackson and Tupac Shakur, to be his best effort. Singleton also wrote and directed other films like Higher Learning (1995), Rosewood (1997), Shaft (2000), Baby Boy (2001), 2 Fast 2 Furious (2003), Four Brothers (2005). Born in 1968, Singleton succumbed from a stroke on April 29, 2019, at age 51.

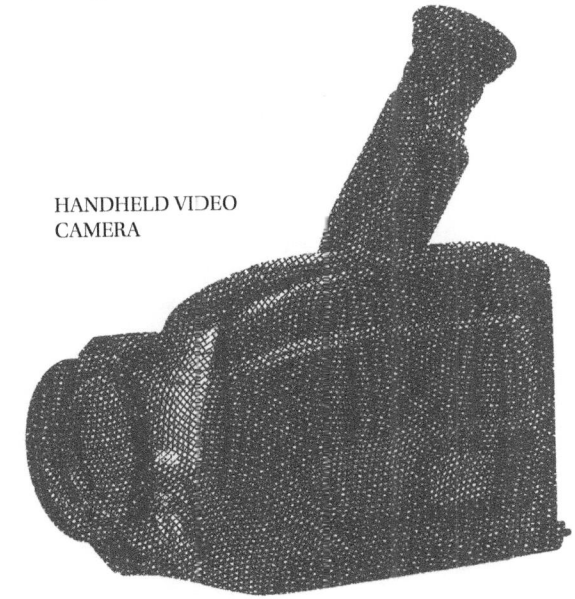

HANDHELD VIDEO CAMERA

ROBERT LEE

FIREFIGHTERS

▪ FIRST BLACK FIREFIGHTER IN LOS ANGELES FIRE DEPARTMENT
▪ FIRST BLACK FIREFIGHTER TO DIE IN THE LINE OF DUTY

In 1895, Sam Haskins, became both the first black firefighter in the Los Angeles Fire Department and the first to die in the line of duty. Haskins was born a slave in 1846 in Virginia and arrived in Los Angeles in 1880. On November 19, 1895, Firefighter Sam Haskins, responded to a 6 p.m. alarm, taking his position on the back of the wagon hauling the steam pump. With the station's mascot, Chief the dog, in the lead, the horse-drawn wagons raced along 1st Street, which was riddled with potholes and street-car tracks, toward Main. When the wagon Haskins was standing on hit a bump, he lost his balance and fell between the wheel and the pump. It took firefighters and passersby more than 10 minutes to take off the wheel to free him. They took him back to the firehouse, where he died a few minutes later. It's important to note that, back in those days, being a volunteer firefighter was very prestigious, and expensive, endeavor. To join the department, volunteer firemen had to have the means to purchase their own personal protective equipment and clothing. (B. 1846 – D. 1895).

▪ FIRST BLACK FIREFIGHTER PROMOTED IN LOS ANGELES FIRE DEPARTMENT

On November 11, 1897, George Bright was promoted to full-time hoseman and assigned to Engine Co. 30. On January 31, 1900, he was promoted to Driver Third Class and assigned to Chemical Engine Co. 1. Before the city would certify his promotions, Bright was required to obtain a letter of endorsement from influential Second Baptist Church. To avoid Bright supervising white firefighters, the department formed the city's first all Black fire company. Bright retired in 1917. (B. Unknown – D. Unknown).

GEORGE BRIGHT AND EDWARD BOWAN

■ FIRST BLACK BATTALION CHIEF IN LOS ANGELES COUNTY FIRE DEPARTMENT
■ FIRST BLACK ASSISTANT FIRE CHIEF IN LOS ANGELES COUNTY FIRE DEPARTMENT
■ FIRST BLACK DEPUTY FIRE CHIEF IN LOS ANGELES COUNTY FIRE DEPARTMENT

In 1984, Chief Robert Lee became the first Black Battalion Chief in the history of the Los Angeles County Fire Department (LACFD). Early in his career, Chief Lee was promoted to firefighter paramedic, firefighter specialist, and captain. Later he was promoted twice to Assistant Fire Chief and then to Deputy Fire Chief, again becoming the first Black person to ever hold those positions in the department. (B. 1945 – D. 2022).

■ FIRST BLACK FIRE CHIEF OF THE LOS ANGELES COUNTY FIRE DEPARTMENT

In February 2011, Daryl Osby was sworn in as the first Black chief of the 4,400-person Los Angeles County Fire Department. On his 2022 retirement Osby said "I am truly grateful for the amazing 38 years I have spent protecting the lives, property, and environment of the residents of Los Angeles County, especially the last eleven in which I had the honor of serving as Fire Chief of the premier fire department in the nation, if not the world." (B. Unknown).

■ FIRST BLACK WOMAN FIRE BATTALION CHIEF IN LOS ANGELES CITY FIRE DEPARTMENT (LAFD)

In 2017, Kristine Larson, a 27-year LAFD veteran, was the first Black woman to be promoted to the rank of battalion chief. LAFD Chief Ralph Terrazas said..."It's an honor to promote Captain Larson. I'm excited to see her embrace her new role overseeing eight fire stations in South LA." (B. 1966).

ROBERT LEE

DARYL OSBY

BRICE UNION TAYLOR

FOOTBALL COACHES

■ FIRST BLACK HIGH SCHOOL HEAD FOOTBALL COACH IN LOS ANGELES

In the early 1940's Brice Union Taylor, USC's first Black football player and LA's first Black college All-American, began coaching football and teaching at Jefferson High School, making him the first Black high school head football coach in Los Angeles. See Football Stars for information on Taylor. (B. 1902 – D. 1974).

■ FIRST BLACK NFL HEAD COACH IN THE MODERN ERA

In 1989, Al Davis owner of the (then) Los Angeles Raiders hired Art Shell, a former Raider player, as Head Coach making Shell the first Black National Football League (NFL) head coach in the modern era. In 1990, the Raiders advanced to the conference championship game with a 12-4 record and Shell became the first Black head coach to lead a team to an NFL Conference Championship game. As a result, Shell was named conference Coach of the Year. Overall, Shell compiled a record of 54 wins, 38 losses. In 1994, Al Davis, the Raiders owner, fired Shell after a 9-7 season. A move Davis later called "a mistake." (B. 1946).

■ FIRST BLACK HEAD FOOTBALL COACH AT UNIVERSITY OF CALIFORNIA LOS ANGELES (UCLA)

In 2002, Karl Dorrell, who played wide receiver for the Bruins in the 1980s, was hired by his alma mater, becoming UCLA's first Black football coach and the fourth Black coach in Division I football. "Obviously, I am privileged and honored to be the new football coach at UCLA," said Dorrell, who landed the job on his 39th birthday. "It has always been a dream of mine to someday return to campus as the head coach at this great university. I can't wait to get started." (B. 1963).

■ FIRST BLACK (INTERIM) HEAD FOOTBALL COACH AT UNIVERSITY OF SOUTHERN CALIFORNIA (USC)

In 2021, USC interim head football coach Donte Williams was named the first Black head coach in Trojans history. Williams had a 3-7 overall record as interim head coach. (B. 1982).

WOODROW "WOODY"
STRODE

FOOTBALL STARS

■ FIRST BLACK COLLEGE FOOTBALL PLAYER AT UNIVERSITY OF SOUTHERN CALIFORNIA (USC)
■ FIRST BLACK COLLEGE FOOTBALL ALL-AMERICAN IN LOS ANGELES

Brice Union Taylor, born without a left hand, showed his athletic prowess while growing up in Seattle, Washington. Taylor played for the USC Trojans football team. He started as a fullback on Gus Henderson's 1924 Trojan team. In 1925, Howard Jones became the new head football coach and moved Taylor to offensive and defensive line and kicker. Taylor played all but four minutes of USC's eleven games that season, a school record that stood for decades. In 1925, Taylor was named LA's first Black college football All-American. (B. 1902 – D. 1974)

■ FIRST BLACK MEN IN NATIONAL FOOTBALL LEAGUE IN THE MODERN ERA

On March 21, 1946, first Kenny Washington and then Woodrow "Woody" Strode - became the first Black players in the National Football League (NFL) in the modern era. From 1899 through 1933, the NFL was an integrated operation and many teams had Black American, Asian-American, Latin American and Native American players on their rosters. However, in 1933 NFL owners banned all Black athletes and instituted segregation. The NFL lifted the ban when the Los Angeles Rams, facing a threat of losing its lease on the Los Angeles Memorial Coliseum unless it ended segregation and included Black players, signed Washington and Strode. Washington (B. 1918 – D. 1971). Strode (B. 1914 – D. 1994).

■ FIRST BLACK HEISMAN TROPHY WINNER IN LOS ANGELES

In 1965, Michael Garrett of the University of Southern California (USC) Trojans won the Heisman Trophy as a halfback making him LA's first Black Heisman Trophy award winner. A two time All-American, Garrett set numerous National Collegiate Athletic Association, Pac-8 Conference and USC records in his career by amassing, a then unheard of, 3,221 yards and scoring 30 touchdowns. Garrett served as USC's athletic director from 1993 until 2010. (B. 1944).

CHAP

PIO PICO MANSION, 1895

TER 7

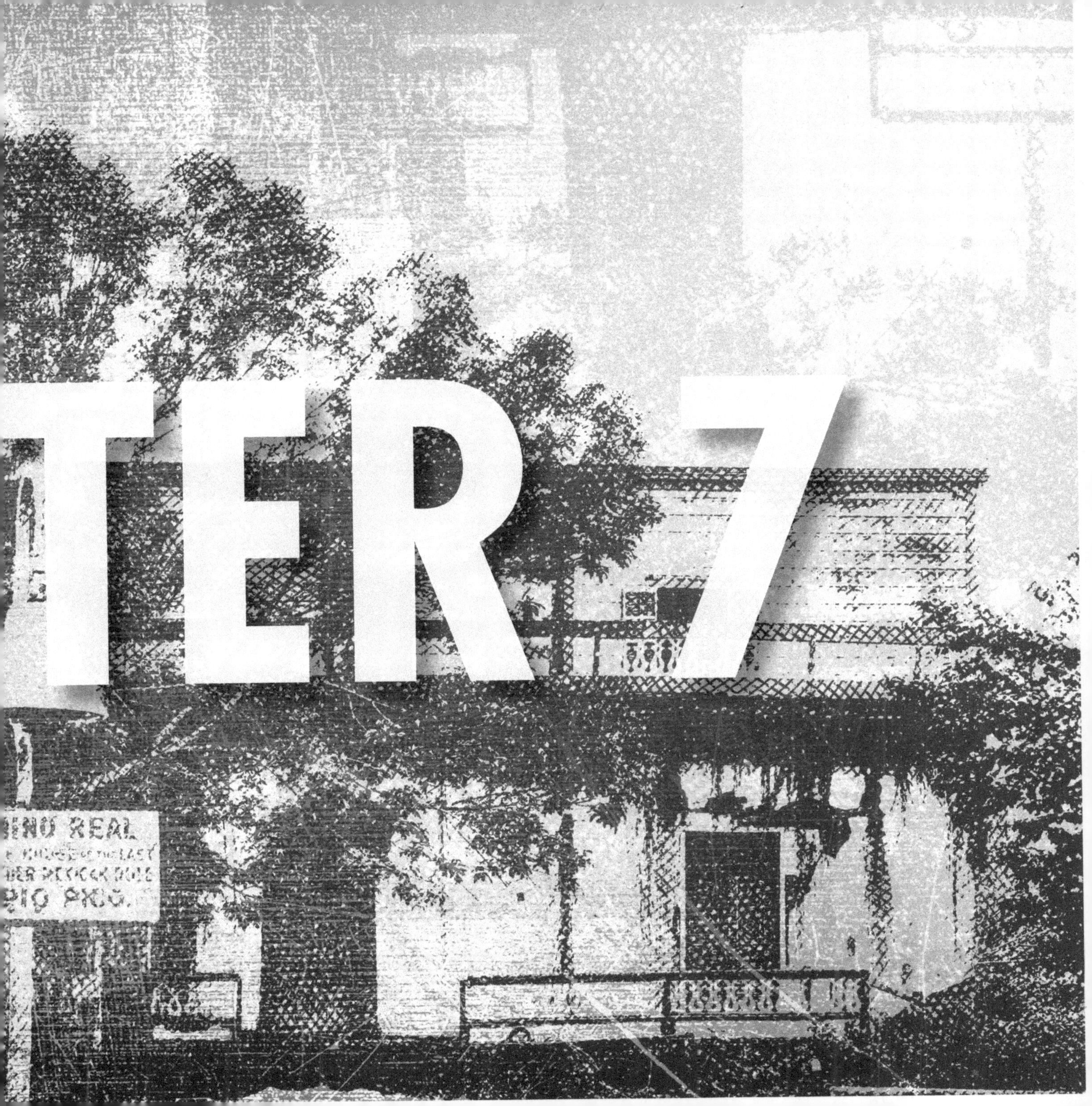

MERYVN DYMALLY

GOVERNOR AND LIEUTENANT GOVERNOR

▪ FIRST BLACK (AFRO-MEXICAN) GOVERNOR OF ALTA CALIFORNIA

In 1845, Pio Pico, a man of Black, Indian, and Spanish ancestry was the first (and last) became Governor of the Mexican state of Alta California serving from 1845 to 1846. His adobe home at "El Ranchito" has been completely restored to how it appeared in the 1800's and can be visited today on a five acre park encompassing historic gardens registered as California Historic Landmark NO. 127.

▪ FIRST BLACK LIEUTENANT GOVERNOR OF CALIFORNIA

In 1974, LA's Meryvn Dymally was elected to the position of Lieutenant Governor making him the first Black person elected to a statewide office in California. See California State *Political Representatives* for more information about Dymally. (B. 1926 – D. 2012).

PIO PICO STATE
HISTORIC PARK

SPRING STREET
COURTHOUSE

GRAND JURY CHAIRPERSON

■ FIRST BLACK CHAIRMAN OF THE LOS ANGELES COUNTY GRAND JURY

In 1974, Jesse Lee Robinson, a Compton civic leader and management expert became the first Black person to chair the Los Angeles County Grand Jury. "Jesse Robinson is one of the greatest guys around," Councilman Maxcy D. Filer said. "In every way—civic, humanitarian, philanthropic—he's the best. Jesse's the type of guy you can debate with, even argue with, and when he leaves the room that's the end of it." In 1987, a small park at the corner of Alameda Street and the Artesia (91) Freeway was renamed in his honor. (B. 1912 – D. 1993).

LADY JUSTICE STATUE

LOS ANGELES COUNTY GENERAL HOSPITAL, 1930

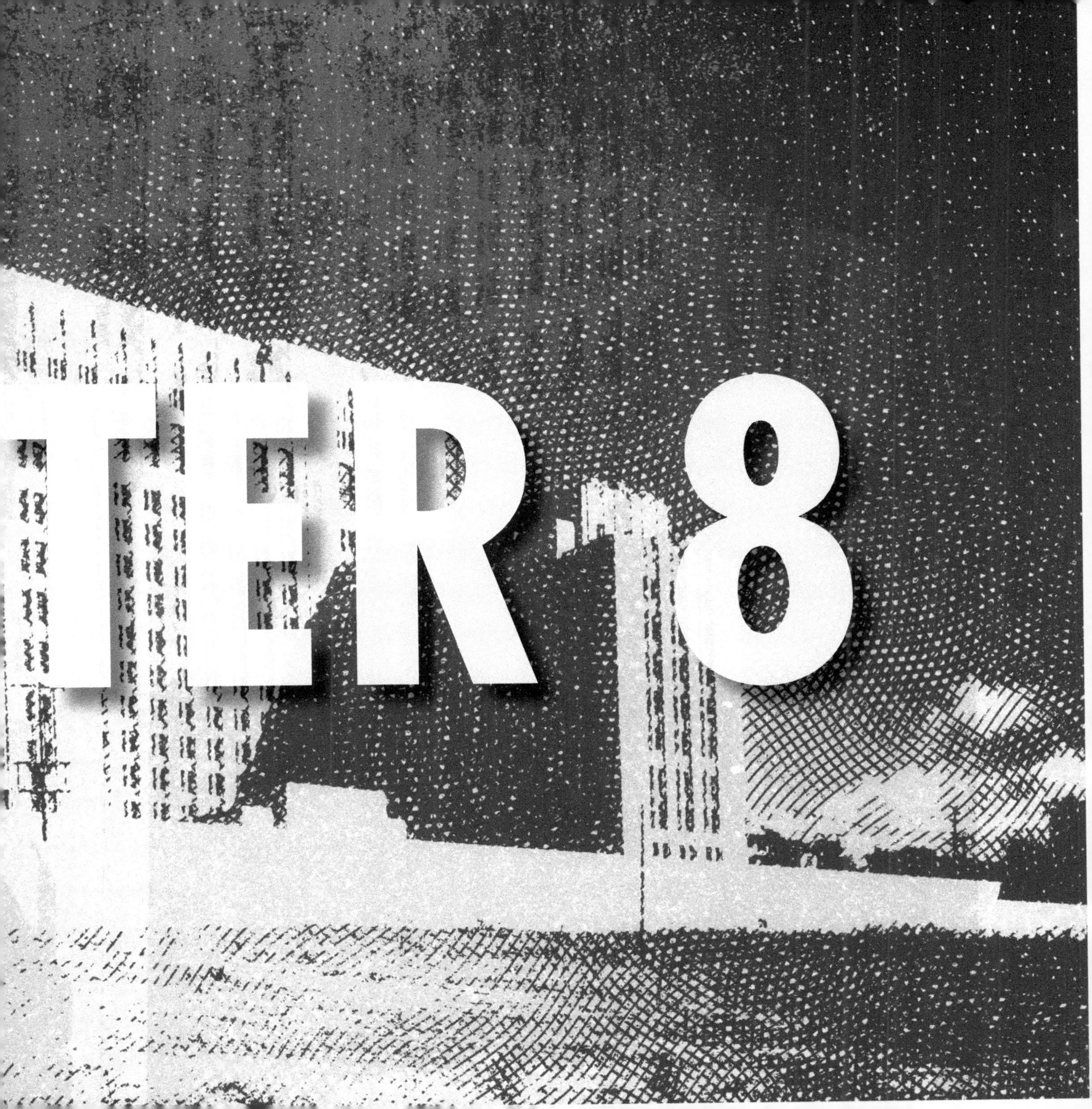
TER 8

LOVIE YANCEY

HAMBURGER QUEEN

■ FIRST BLACK HAMBURGER QUEEN

In 1947, Lovie Yancey founded the first Fatburger hamburger stand on Western Ave. in South Los Angeles (LA). From the beginning, Yancey, whose customers included entertainers such as Redd Foxx and Ray Charles, worked 16 hours a day behind the counter, seven days a week. In 1973, Yancey opened a Fatburger on La Cienega Boulevard in Beverly Hills and it became a favorite destination for celebrity burger buffs. Over the years, Fatburger has been immortalized in songs, movies and TV shows, including the sitcom Sanford and Son, the film The Fast and the Furious and the Ice Cube single It Was a Good Day. In 1981, Yancey began offering franchises, and by 1985, in addition to four company locations, there were 15 Fatburger franchise sites. For three consecutive years, beginning in 1985, Fatburger was named in Entrepreneur magazine's annual Franchise 500 list. Yancey sold her Fatburger company to an investment group in 1990 but retained control of the original property on Western Avenue. (B. 1912 – D. 2008).

HEAD OF HOUSEHOLD

■ FIRST BLACK HEAD OF HOUSEHOLD LISTED IN UNITED STATES (U.S.) CENSUS OF LOS ANGELES

The U.S. Census of 1850 identified two Black American households in the city of Los Angeles (LA). Of those, Peter Biggs was the only Black person listed as a "head of household" in the official record. See *Barbershop Owner* to learn more about Biggs. (B. Unknown – D. Unknown).

ANTHONY M. PACHOT

HELICOPTER PILOTS

■ FIRST BLACK HELICOPTER PILOT IN LOS ANGELES COUNTY SHERIFF'S DEPARTMENT

In the 1980's, Anthony M. Pachot became the Los Angeles County Sheriff's department (LACSD) first Black helicopter pilot. After joining LACSD in 1975, Pachot worked as a jailer, a patrol deputy at the Firestone station, and a detective. Later, because he had a pilot's license, Pachot applied for work LACSD's Aero Bureau located in the city of Long Beach. Pachot retired in 2008 after 20 years as a sheriff's pilot. (B. 1947 – D. 2013).

■ FIRST BLACK HELICOPTER PILOT IN LONG BEACH POLICE DEPARTMENT

In the early 1990's Corporal Michael Colbert was hired by the Long Beach Police Department (LBPD) making him LBPD's first and only Black helicopter pilot. Colbert experienced malicious overt racism and discrimination on a daily basis stating "I had to walk into the office every day and be reminded of that and how inferior they thought I was." In a court case, Colbert details racial animus from fellow officers who used epithets on the job, including the n-word, created a hostile work environment and repeatedly demeaned him in uniform and in public. (B. 1969).

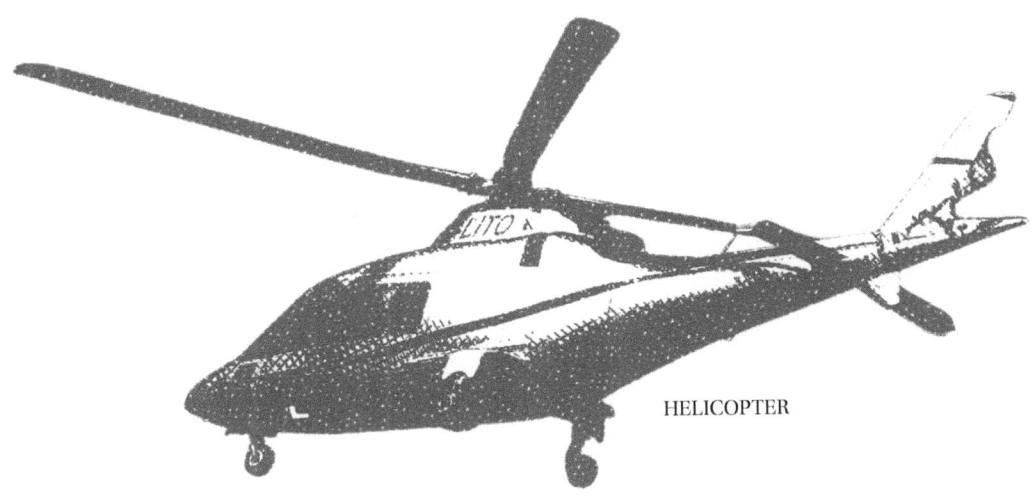

HELICOPTER

MAGIC JOHNSON

HIGHWAY PATROLMAN

■ FIRST BLACK OFFICER HIRED BY THE CALIFORNIA HIGHWAY PATROL

In 1942, Homer L. Garrott became the first Black California Highway Patrol (CHP) officer. He was assigned to the East Los Angeles division and remained the only Black officer with the CHP for years. Shortly after he was hired, a small group of community members, led by a local newspaper, petitioned the CHP for Garrott's removal. However, despite their efforts, the CHP stood by him. (B. 1915 – D. 1998). See *Motorcycle Officer* to learn more about Garrott.

HIV+ PRO ATHLETE

■ FIRST HIV+ ATHLETE IN PRO SPORTS

On September 30, 1992, Magic Johnson, whose HIV induced retirement from basketball in 1991 stunned the nation, rejoined the Los Angeles Lakers, making him the first HIV+ athlete in pro sports. Johnson said "I'm not going to sit here and say you're not going to run a risk, but life itself is a risk. But to have that fun and be out there, I'll take it and I know everything is going to be all right." (B. 1959).

HOMER L. GARROTT

FAY M. JACKSON

HOLLYWOOD CORRESPONDENT

■ **FIRST BLACK HOLLYWOOD CORRESPONDENT**
■ **FIRST BLACK FOREIGN CORRESPONDENT**

a University of Southern California journalism graduate, was born on May 8, 1902 in Dallas, Texas and moved to Los Angeles, California in 1922. By the age of twenty-six years Jackson had acquired the foundation needed to turn into an entrepreneur, a two-fisted reporter deeply concerned about the political welfare of her community, and a revolutionary voice in the Black press. Jackson started the first Black intellectual newsweekly on the west coast entitled Flash in 1928; became the political editor of the California Eagle in 1931, and served as the first Hollywood correspondent for the Associated Negro Press (ANP) in the 1930s.

Her work as the first Black female foreign correspondent for the ANP in 1937 remains her most important contribution to the Black press. Little work exists, however, on her life and achievements in this . Please arena; hence Jackson remains a part of a forgotten legacy of Black female pioneers in the field of foreign journalism. (B. 1902 – D. 1979). See *Newspaper Journalist* for more information on Jackson.

VINTAGE
TYPEWRITTER

WEST VIEW HOSPITAL
RENDERING BY PAUL WILLIAMS

HOSPITALS

■ FIRST BLACK-OWNED PRIVATE HOSPITAL IN LOS ANGELES

In 1923, Dr. Richard S. Whittaker, in response to the discrimination practiced by hospitals against Black patients in Los Angeles, established The Dunbar Hospital, a small 20 bed facility located at 1393 E. 15th Street (the building has been demolished). Dunbar Hospital operated until 1938 providing a collegial atmosphere for the doctors and a modern medical facility for LA's growing Black community. When that facility closed, the West View Hospital Association, a coalition of Black health professionals and community members, began raising funds for a new hospital. The association purchased a property on Main Street and made plans for a modern 300-bed hospital in South Los Angeles. However, because adequate funding never materialized, the facilities were not completed and the project was abandoned in 1952.

■ FIRST INTERRACIAL HOSPITAL IN LOS ANGELES

Dr. Norris Curtis King, a 1924 graduate of Meharry Medical School, moved his family to Los Angeles in 1929. In 1941, King founded the Rose-Netta Hospital, one of the first truly interracial hospitals in the United States. The hospital served, and employed, people of all races/ethnicities including Blacks, Mexicans, Japanese and Whites. Dr. King was also head of the Los Angeles Venereal Clinic and several other clinics.

BLACK NURSE

JESSIE L. TERRY

HOUSING SPECIALIST

■ FIRST BLACK PERSON ON THE LOS
ANGELES HOUSING COMMISSION
■ FIRST WOMAN TO MANAGE A CITY
HOUSING PROJECT IN LOS ANGELES

On June 21, 1939 Jessie L. Terry became the first Black person appointed to the Housing Authority of the City of Los Angeles (HACLA). In 1940, under Terry's leadership, HACLA's Advisory Committee on Tenant Selection met with City authorities and advocated that HACLA should create integrated housing projects, circumventing United States Housing Authority guidelines designed to foster segregation. In 1943, HACLA rescinded its racial quota policy based on the existing population of the community.

Once these anti-segregation policies had been established under Terry, HACLA was said to have "the most enlightened, liberal and complete inter-racial policy to be effected anywhere in public housing," according to the National Committee Against Discrimination in Housing. Terry served in the role through January 6, 1944. Later, Terry became the first Black person to manage a Los Angeles city housing project. (B. 1885 – D. 1973).

NICKERSON GARDENS,
WATTS

115

CHAP

UCLA MEDICAL CENTER CIRCA 1950s

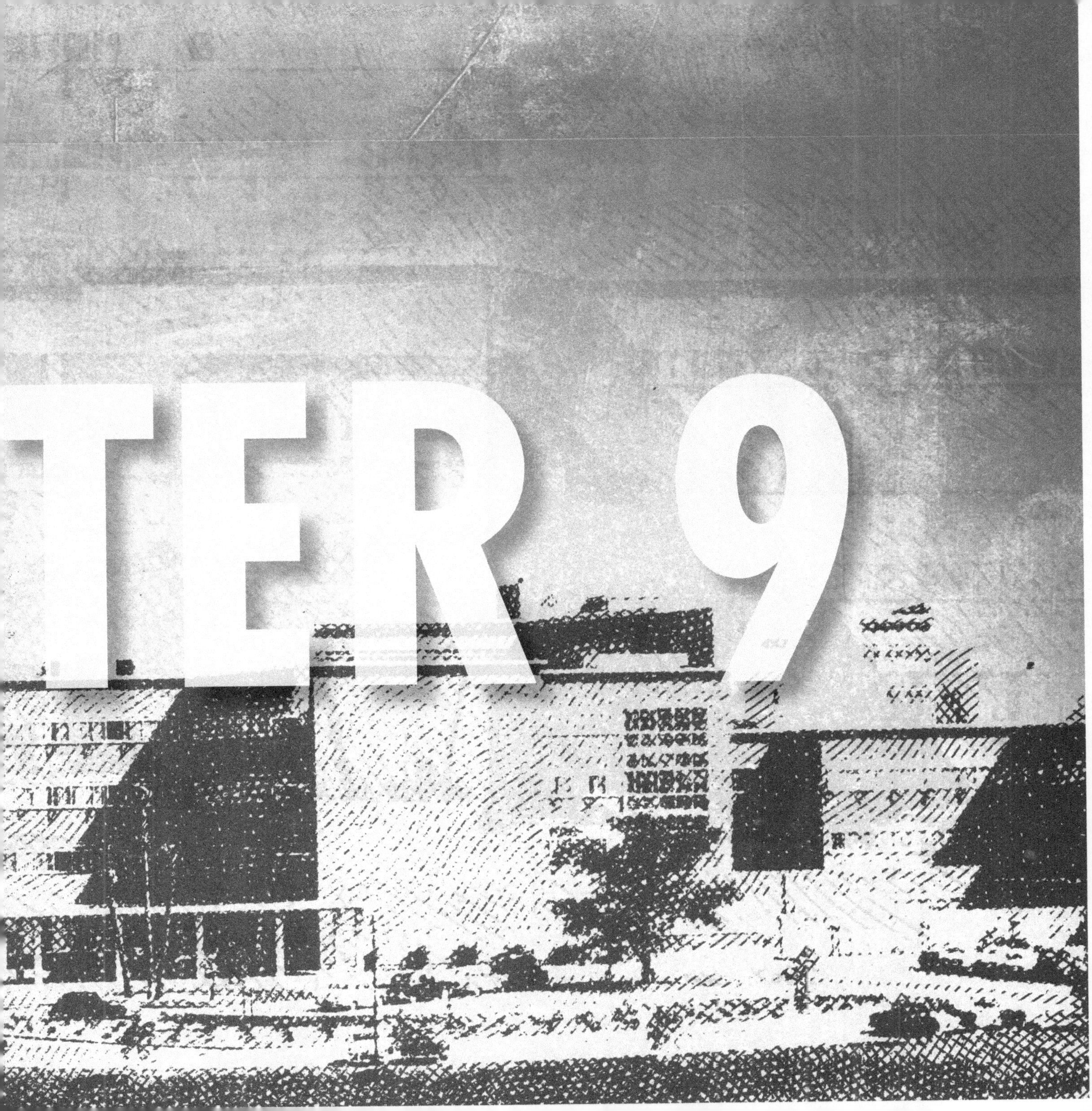
TER 9

PATRICIA BATH

INVENTOR

■ FIRST BLACK WOMAN AWARDED MEDICAL PATENT

In 1973, Dr. Patricia Bath became the first Black doctor to complete a residency in ophthalmology. In 1974, she moved from New York to California to work as an assistant professor of surgery at both Charles R. Drew University and UCLA. In 1975, Bath became the first female faculty member in the Department of Ophthalmology at UCLA's Jules Stein Eye Institute. In 1976, she co-founded the American Institute for the Prevention of Blindness, which established that "eyesight is a basic human right." By 1981, Bath had began working on her most well-known invention: the Laserphaco Probe. In 1983, Bath helped create the Ophthalmology Residency Training program at UCLA-Drew, which she also chaired, becoming, in addition to her other firsts, the first woman in the nation to hold such a position.

By 1986, Bath, harnessing laser technology to create a less painful and more precise instrument for treating cataracts, had completed the Laserphaco Probe. Bath patented the device in 1988, becoming the first Black female doctor to receive a medical patent. Ultimately, the device helped to restore and improve vision for millions of cataract patients. (B. 1942 – D. 2019).

PATRICIA BATH
PATENT

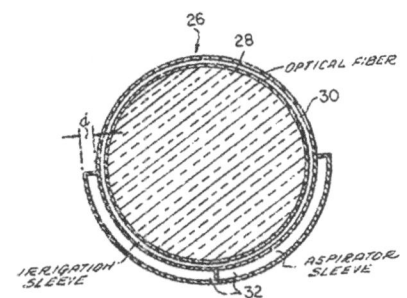

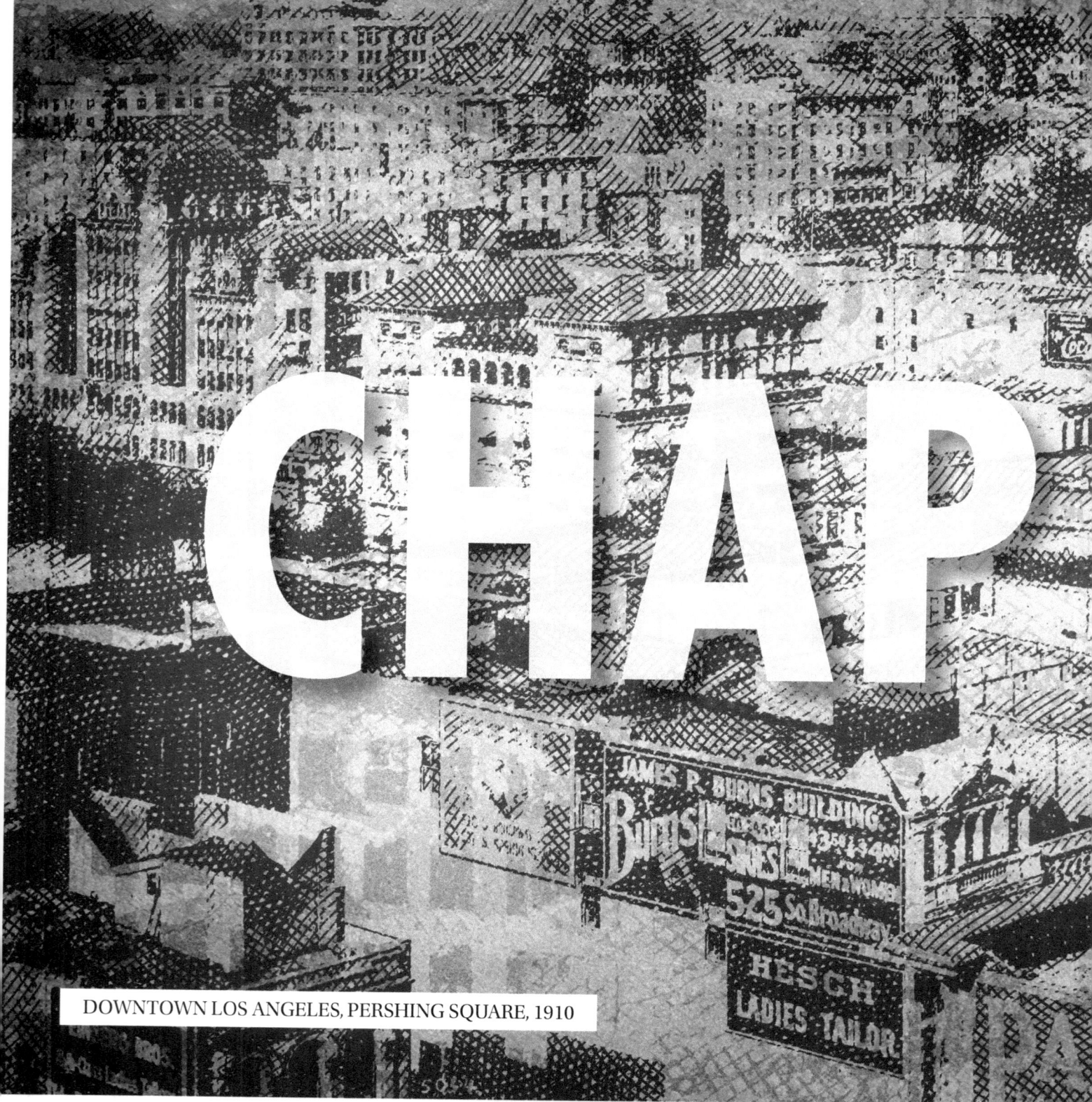

CHAP

DOWNTOWN LOS ANGELES, PERSHING SQUARE, 1910

JOHN W. COLEMAN

JANITOR

■ FIRST BLACK JANITOR HIRED BY LOS ANGELES COUNTY

Lewis Gomez Green, a former slave, served in the United States military during the Mexican-American war and settled in Los Angeles (LA) shortly afterwards. In 1869, he opened the second Black-owned barbershop in the city. In 1874, attorney Robert M. Widney successfully petitioned the LA County Board of Supervisors to appoint Green to the position of janitor. Green was referred to as the colored janitor of the county courthouse. (B. Unknown – D. Unknown). See *Civil Rights Activist* to learn more about Green.

■ FIRST AND ONLY BLACK JANITOR TO BECOME LOS ANGELES CITY COUNCIL MEMBER

In 1963, Gilbert W. Lindsay, the flamboyant politician, the self-proclaimed Emperor of the Great 9th District, became the first, and so far only, person to work their way from city janitor to become LA's first Black city Council member and one of its most powerful local elected officials. Lindsay had become a political force commanding the attention and respect of power brokers, whom he had once cleaned up after while working as a janitor. (B. 1900 – D. 1990).

JOB KING

■ FIRST BLACK EMPLOYMENT KING

In 1887, after working as a Pullman Porter and traveling the country by rail, John Wesley Coleman settled in Los Angeles. Coleman became a successful real estate investor and civic leader. In 1907, he opened LA's first Black employment agency that helped so many newcomers find jobs that Coleman became known as LA's employment king. (B. 1865 – D. 1930).

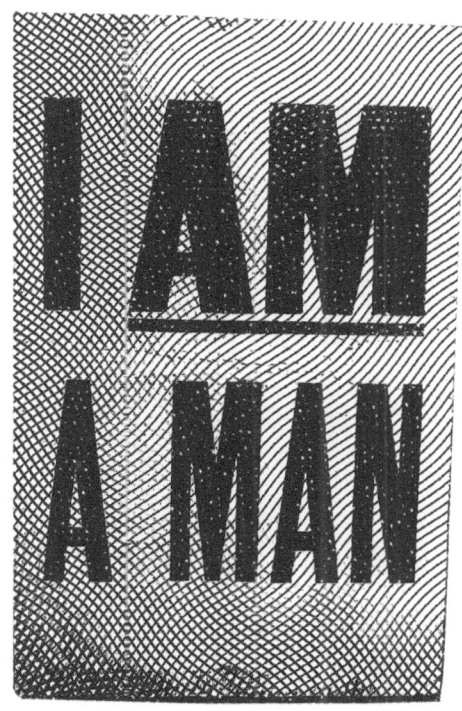

I AM A MAN POSTER

VAINO SPENCER

JUDGES

■ FIRST BLACK PERSON APPOINTED TO A CALIFORNIA MUNICIPAL COURT

In 1953, the Honorable Thomas Griffith Jr., the son of Thomas Griffith Sr., the senior minister of South Los Angeles' influential Second Baptist Church and the first Black lawyer admitted to the Los Angeles (LA) Bar Association, was appointed to the California Municipal Court in LA by, then, California Governor Earl Warren. (B. 1903 – D. 1986).

■ FIRST BLACK WOMAN APPOINTED JUDGE IN CALIFORNIA

In 1961, the Honorable Vaino Spencer became the first Black woman appointed to a judgeship in California (Los Angeles Municipal Court) making her the first Black woman appointed to the judiciary in California. In 1976, Spencer was named to the Superior Court and, in 1980, named Presiding Justice of California Court of Appeal (Second District). (B. 1920 – D. 2016).

■ FIRST BLACK PERSON ELECTED PRESIDING JUDGE OF THE LOS ANGELES MUNICIPAL COURT

In 1961, Thomas Griffith Jr, was elected presiding judge of the Municipal Court, the first Black man so honored by his peers.

■ FIRST BLACK PERSON ELECTED TO THE LOS ANGELES SUPERIOR COURT

In November 1968, Thomas Griffith Jr., was elected to Superior Court, the first Black judge chosen by county voters.

■ FIRST BLACK WOMAN APPOINTED TO CALIFORNIA COURT OF APPEAL

In 1980, the Honorable Arleigh M. Woods, the youngest woman admitted to the California Bar Association, became the first Black woman appointed to be a Justice of the California Court of Appeal (Second Appellate District) and the first to any state appeal court in the United States. (B. 1929 – D. 2022).

FIRST BLACK WOMAN APPOINTED PRESIDING JUDGE OF LOS ANGELES MUNICIPAL COURT

In 1987, the Honorable Maxine F. Thomas became the first Black woman appointed as presiding judge of the Los Angeles (LA) Municipal Court. Born and raised in South-Central LA, Thomas quickly became a rising star in town with backers like then-Supervisor Kenneth Hahn and then-Councilmember Gilbert Lindsay. In 1980, at age 32, Thomas was appointed to the Municipal Court bench by then-Governor Jerry Brown. Upon her death at age 50 state Senator Diane Watson said "we have lost one of the youngest and most brilliant female attorneys and judges. Her life may have been short, but it was distinguished. (B. 1938 – D. 1998).

FIRST BLACK MALE TO SERVE AS THE PRESIDING JUDGE OF THE LOS ANGELES COUNTY SUPERIOR COURT

On September 15, 2019, Judge Kevin C. Brazile became the first Black person to be elected presiding judge of the Superior Court of Los Angeles County, the largest trial court system in the nation. In 1980, Brazile earned a Bachelor of Arts in political science from the University of California Los Angeles (UCLA) and a Juris Doctor from the UCLA School of Law in 1983. Prior to his current role, Brazile served as a civil trial attorney for the Los Angeles (LA) County Counsel's office from 1984 through 2002 and was appointed to the LA Superior Court in 2003. (B. Unknown).

FIRST BLACK PERSON APPOINTED TO VOTING POSITION ON LOS ANGELES COUNTY SUPERIOR COURT JUDICIAL COUNCIL

On September 15, 2020, Judge Kevin C. Brazile became the first Black person appointed to a voting position on the Los Angeles County Superior Court Judicial Council. When asked what the experience meant to him Brazile said, "opportunity, appreciation, gratitude and a way to give back to the community and to the people who have helped me and supported me throughout my life."

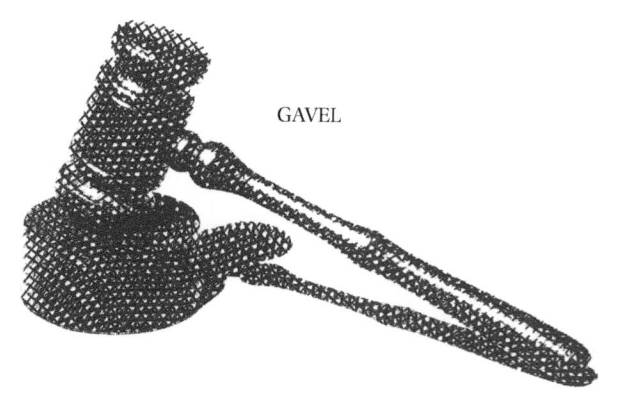

GAVEL

KEVIN C. BRAZILE

ANN SHAW

JUDICIAL OVERSEER

■ FIRST BLACK PERSON ON CALIFORNIA COMMISSION ON JUDICIAL PERFORMANCE

In 1975, Ann Shaw was appointed to serve on the California Commission on Judicial Performance by then-Governor of California, Jerry Brown making her both the first woman and first Black person responsible for judicial oversight in the state. The Commission on Judicial Performance, established in 1960, is the independent state agency responsible for investigating complaints of judicial misconduct and judicial incapacity and for disciplining judges, pursuant to article VI, section 18 of the California Constitution. The commission's mandate is to protect the public, enforce rigorous standards of judicial conduct and maintain public confidence in the integrity and independence of the judicial system. While the majority of California's judges are committed to maintaining the high standards expected of the judiciary, an effective method of disciplining judges who engage in misconduct is essential to the functioning of our judicial system. Commission proceedings provide a fair and appropriate mechanism to preserve the integrity of the judicial process. The commission's jurisdiction includes all judges of California's superior courts and the justices of the Court of Appeal and Supreme Court.

Shaw was the first Black person to lead the Young Women's Christian Association of Greater Los Angeles. Over the course of her career, Shaw served on many boards and received numerous awards and honors including the United Way's highest award, the Gold Key Award, National Association for the Advancement of Colored People Legal Defense Fund's Black Woman of Achievement Award (1985), and was named Woman of the Year by the Los Angeles (LA) Times (1969), LA Sentinel (1964) and the California State Legislature. In 1968, Shaw earned a Masters of Social Work degree from the University of Southern California. Shaw's husband, Leslie N. Shaw, was LA's first Black postmaster. (B. 1921 – D. 2015).

CHAP

LOOKING NORTH OVER CRENSHAW CENTER, 1946

SIJO STEVE MUHAMMAD

KARATE SCHOOLS

▌ FIRST BLACK KARATE SCHOOL IN LOS ANGELES

William Short, an imposing six-foot, four-inches and two-hundred and seventy-eight pounds, became one of the first Black Americans to earn a black belt in shotokan karate overseas. He returned to Los Angeles in the late 1950s and opened the Kobayashi School of Karate on So. Western Ave. (B. Unknown – D. Unknown).

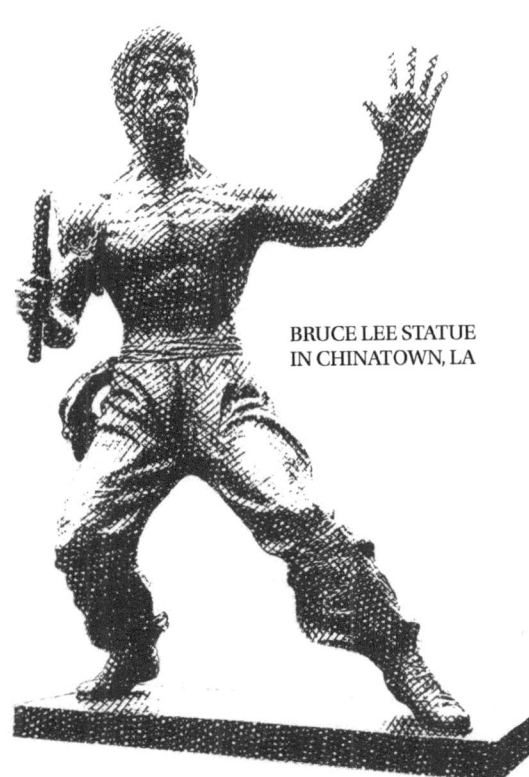

BRUCE LEE STATUE
IN CHINATOWN, LA

▌ FIRST BLACK KARATE FEDERATION IN LOS ANGELES

In 1969, a group of Black martial artists (Sijo Steve Sanders Muhammad, Cliff Stewart, Jerry Smith, Ron Chapel, Donnie Williams, Karl Armelin and Curtis Pulliam) started training on Saturdays at Van Ness Park attracting dozens of other martial artists. Eventually these gatherings led to the formation of the Black Karate Federation (BKF). Open to all races the BKF, was established as a backlash against the unfair treatment Black competitors faced in some martial arts tournaments. Sanders served as the organizations first president. In 1970, BKF opened the 103rd Street School in South Central Los Angeles. In 1973, a scene from the classic martial arts film Enter the Dragon starring Bruce Lee that featured Sanders and Williams was filmed inside the original BKF studio on 103rd Street. In 1976, they opened another school at 42nd and Crenshaw Blvd. which has continuously operated since then and remains open today. Sanders Muhammad (B. 1939). Williams (B. 1947). Stewart (B. Unknown). Smith (B. Unknown). Chapel (B. Unknown). Armelin (B. Unknown). Pulliam (B. Unknown).

CHAP

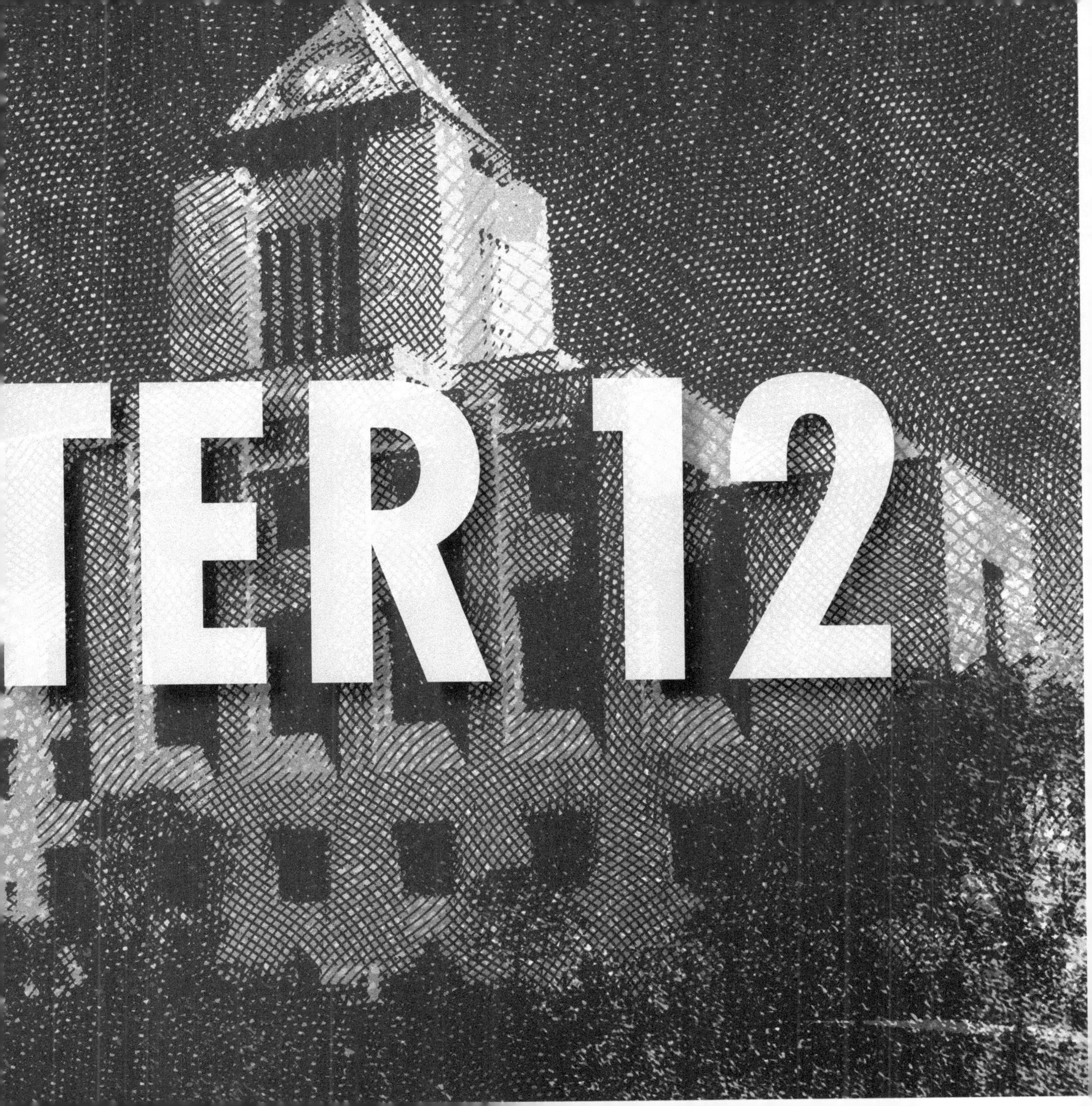
TER 12

YVONNE
WHEELER

LABOR LEADERS

■ FIRST INTEGRATED MUSIC UNION

In 1951, jazz flutist, saxophonist, and clarinetist, William "Buddy" Collette became the first Black musician in a West Coast Television Studio Band. At that time, LA's music unions were segregated. Collette became a leading activist against racism and discrimination in the music industry, leading efforts to form one, color-blind music union. In 1953, he was successful in achieving the merger of LA's Black and white music unions. (B. 1921 – D. 2010). See *Musicians* for more information on Collette.

■ FIRST BLACK EXECUTIVE VICE PRESIDENT OF THE AFL-CIO

Arlene Holt Baker began her work in the labor movement in Los Angeles in 1972. Baker worked as a union area director for the American Federation of State, County and Municipal Employees from 1980s until the mid-90s. In 1995, Baker joined the American Federation of Labor–Congress of Industrial Organizations (AFL-CIO) as executive assistant to the vice president. In 2007, upon the retirement of her predecessor, Baker was approved to serve in her former boss' role. in 2009, Baker was elected to a full term as executive vice president and served the federation until her retirement in 2013. (B. 1951).

■ FIRST BLACK WOMAN TO HEAD LOS ANGELES COUNTY FEDERATION OF LABOR

In November 2022, veteran labor leader Yvonne Wheeler took over as head of the Los Angeles County Federation of Labor, becoming the first Black woman to lead the powerful group in its nearly 140-year history. Wheeler was tasked with repairing the institution's relationship with Black workers and building solidarity with Latino workers. (B. Unknown).

ARLENE HOLT BAKER

THOMAS GRIFFITH JR.

SAMUEL L.
WILLIAMS

LAWYERS

▮ FIRST BLACK MALE LAWYER IN LOS ANGELES

Robert Charles O'Hara Benjamin's name has been etched in history books under numerous "firsts," including the first Black lawyer in Virginia and Alabama. In 1884, Benjamin became the first Black lawyer to practice law in California courts and the first Black editor of numerous newspapers. Although he may not have been the first Black editor or the first Black lawyer, he's the one we know of. We need to remember him and people like him. Benjamin died at age 45 when he was beaten to death for helping register black voters by white men who opposed his efforts. (B. 1885 – D. 1900).

▮ FIRST BLACK ATTORNEY ADMITTED TO LOS ANGELES COUNTY BAR ASSOCIATION

In 1950, attorney Thomas Griffith Jr., the son of Thomas Griffith Sr., the senior minister of South Los Angeles' influential Second Baptist Church, became the first Black member of the Los Angeles County Bar Association. (B. 1903 – D. 1986).

▮ FIRST BLACK PRESIDENT OF THE STATE BAR OF CALIFORNIA
▮ FIRST BLACK MALE PRESIDENT OF THE LOS ANGELES COUNTY BAR ASSOCIATION

In 1977, attorney Samuel L. Williams became the first Black male to serve as the president of the Los Angeles County Bar Association. In 1981, he became the first Black president of the State Bar of California. Earlier in his career, Williams was a staff attorney for the McCone Commission, which investigated the 1965 Watts riots and was on the Police Commission when it voted to suspend Chief Daryl F. Gates in the aftermath of the Rodney G. King beating. He played football and baseball at University of California, Berkeley while also being named an Academic All-American. After graduating from the University of Southern California, School of Law, Williams worked as a probation officer and deputy state attorney general before entering private practice. (B. 1933 – D. 1994).

BILLY G. MILLS

HELEN WHEELER
RIDDLE

LAW SCHOOL GRADUATES

■ FIRST BLACK USC LAW SCHOOL GRADUATE

In 1904, Clarence B. Thompson became the first Black person to graduate from the USC Law School. (B. 1882 – D. 1969)

■ FIRST BLACK FEMALE USC LAW SCHOOL GRADUATE

In 1927, Helen W. Riddle became the first Black woman to graduate from the USC School of Law. (B. 1904 – D. 1956).

■ FIRST BLACK UCLA LAW SCHOOL GRADUATE

In 1954, Billy G. Mills became the first Black person to graduate from the UCLA School of Law. In 1963, Mills was among the first three Black people elected to serve on the Los Angeles City Council. (B. 1929). See *City Council Members* to learn more about Mills.

UCLA SCHOOL OF LAW

MIRIAM MATTHEWS

LIBRARIAN

LIFEGUARD

■ FIRST BLACK LIBRARIAN IN THE LOS ANGELES PUBLIC LIBRARY SYSTEM

In July 1927, Miriam Matthews became the first Black credentialed librarian in California, and the first hired by the Los Angeles Public Library (LAPL). Matthews identified "a small collection of books on the Negro" and began building that into a substantial research collection documenting the contributions made by Black people to California's history and culture, which she shared with librarians, researchers and other users. (B. 1905 – D. 2003).

■ FIRST BLACK LIFEGUARD IN LOS ANGELES COUNTY

In 1965, Russell Walker became LA County's first Black lifeguard. "I've been called so many firsts before in my career," said Walker, who recently was promoted to captain and placed in charge of the county Lifeguard Division's Central Section in Santa Monica. "In fact, each time I'm promoted, I am the first." Walker said, "my personal goal is to get more minorities and women into our workforce and provide programs and activities that would help them develop their swimming skills so that we would have a recruitment pool to choose from." (B. Unknown).

LOS ANGELES PUBLIC LIBRARY

SOUTHERN PACIFIC DEPOT (NOW UNION STATION) 1918

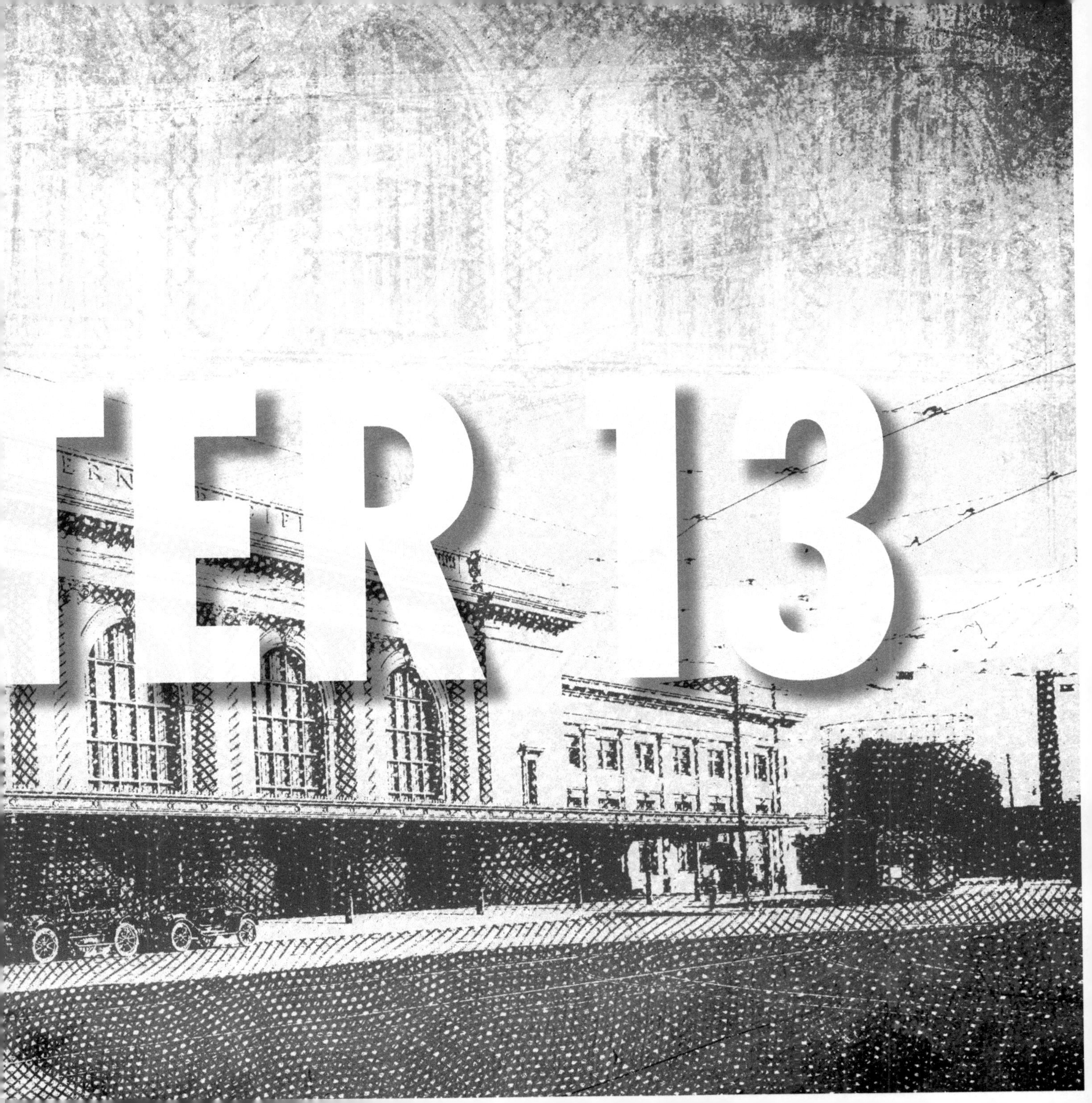
ER 13

The Sweet Smell of Success Coopers MARCH 6th

LOS ANGELES MARATHON

MARATHON ORGANIZER

■ FIRST BLACK PERSON TO ORGANIZE A MARATHON IN LOS ANGELES

William Burke was the catalyst behind the first Los Angeles Marathon. In 1984, after the LA City Council passed a resolution to organize a marathon and began to solicit proposals, Burke, a successful businessperson, and the husband of former Congresswoman and former LA County Supervisor, Yvonne Braithwaite Burke, was soon at the microphone, across from his old City Hall friends, smiling and waving his own proposal. In 1986, Burke's Los Angeles Marathon Inc was ready to rock and roll.

By most measures, the first marathon was a success. Burke had hoped for 2,500 runners; he got nearly 11,000, the largest first-time field for a marathon. The course linked 16 distinct communities, including the Crenshaw District, Chinatown, Exposition Park, Hollywood, Koreatown and Mid-Wilshire. KCOP-TV's coverage of the race pulled the highest ratings for a single program in the station's existence. (B. 1939).

MARATHON WINNER, SIMON NJOROGE

147

EDWARD
VINCENT

MAYORS

■ FIRST BLACK (AFRO-HISPANIC) MAYOR OF LOS ANGELES

In 1793, arriving in Los Angeles shortly after the city's settlement, Juan Francisco Reyes, a mulatto soldier from Zapotlán el Grande in Jalisco became both the first Black and the first Hispanic alcalde (or mayor) of Los Angeles. Reyes served from 1793 to 1795. Reyes was also the Spanish Crown's first land grantee and the original grantee of the San Fernando Rancho - now the San Fernando Valley. (B. 1749 – D. 1809).

■ FIRST BLACK MAYOR OF COMPTON

Douglas Dollarhide lived through the transformation of Compton from a virulently racist all-White city into one of the most heavily concentrated African American suburbs in the United States. In 1969, when Dollarhide was elected mayor, he was the first Black mayor of a major town in California since Americans ruled the state. Dollarhide served one term (1969–1973). During his tenure, the city became the first municipality in California to have a Black majority; and, by 1970, Black people comprised 65 percent of the population. (B. 1923 – D. 2008).

■ FIRST BLACK WOMAN ELECTED MAYOR OF COMPTON

In 1973, Doris A. Davis became the first Black woman mayor of Compton. Davis served from 1973–1977. (B. 1935).

■ FIRST BLACK AMERICAN MAYOR OF LOS ANGELES

In 1973, Los Angeles City Councilman Tom Bradley defeated incumbent Sam Yorty to become the second Black person and first Black American to become mayor of the City of Los Angeles. (B. 1917 – D. 1998).

TOM BRADLEY

▮ FIRST BLACK MAYOR OF INGLEWOOD

In November 1983, Edward Vincent won Inglewood's mayoral election making him the city's first Black mayor. Vincent served in that role for 13 years before entering state politics. (B. 1934 – D. 2012).

▮ FIRST BLACK MAYOR OF LONG BEACH

On November 15, 2022, Rex Richardson, Long Beach's vice mayor and council member for the 9th District, was elected, making him the city's first Black mayor. Richardson said Long beach is unique. "It is not often you hear stories like mine, where someone can come here as a young man, become the youngest City Council member, become the youngest vice mayor and break barriers as the first Black mayor. Long Beach is a special city like that." (B. 1983).

▮ FIRST WOMAN ELECTED MAYOR OF LOS ANGELES

On November 16, 2022, Karen Bass won the Los Angeles mayoral race making her the first woman, third Black person and second Black American elected to lead the city in its 241-year history. (B. 1953). See *California State Political Representatives From LA* for more information about Bass.

REX RICHARDSON

150

KAREN BASS

CHARLES DREW

MEDICAL SCHOOL

∎ FIRST BLACK MEDICAL SCHOOL WEST OF THE MISSISSIPPI

Charles Drew University of Medicine and Science was incorporated in the State of California as a private, nonprofit educational institution in 1966 in response to the McCone Commission's recommendations to improve access to healthcare in South Los Angeles following the Watts Riots in 1965. In 1973, Governor Ronald Reagan signed Senate Bill 1026 authored by State Senator Mervyn Dymally to allocate funding and support for the institution. In January 1970, the offices of the Charles R. Drew Postgraduate Medical School and the Watts-Willowbrook Regional Medical

program formally opened at 12012 Compton Avenue however; the medical school was run in partnership with UCLA. On October 18, 2022, Charles Drew University, LA's only historically Black university, received approval to start its own independent medical school. The only other historically Black colleges and universities to have a medical program are Morehouse College in Atlanta, Meharry Medical College in Nashville, and Howard University in Washington, D.C.

CHARLES DREW UNIVERSITY
OF MEDICINE AND SCIENCE

RUTH JANETTA TEMPLE

MEDICAL SCHOOL FACULTY

■ FIRST BLACK MEDICAL SCHOOL FACULTY MEMBER TO TEACH MEDICINE TO WHITE MEDICAL STUDENTS IN THE UNITED STATES

In 1933, Dr. Ruth Janetta Temple held a teaching position at White Memorial Hospital in Los Angeles likely making her the first Black medical school teacher in the United States. (B. 1892 – D. 1984). See *Doctors* and *Professor* for more information about Temple.

■ FIRST WOMAN IN THE UNITED STATES APPOINTED TO CHAIR OPHTHALMOLOGY DEPARTMENT

In 1983, Dr. Patricia Bath, the first female medical school faculty member in the Department of Ophthalmology at UCLA's Jules Stein Eye Institute, was appointed Chair of the Ophthalmology Residency Program at Charles R. Drew University-UCLA making her the first Black chairperson of an Ophthalmology program in the United States. (B. 1942 – D. 2019). See *Inventor* for more information about Bath.

TEXTBOOKS

DOROTHY DANDRIDGE

MIDWIFE

■ FIRST DOCUMENTED BLACK MIDWIFE IN LOS ANGELES

In the late-1850's, Biddy Mason became the first documented Black midwife in Los Angeles (LA). Mason helped deliver hundreds of babies in early LA. See Churches, Property Owners, and School for more information about Mason. (B. 1818 – D. 1891).

MODEL

■ FIRST BLACK MODEL FEATURED ON THE COVER OF A WHITE MAGAZINE

In 1954, Dorothy Dandridge, a woman of exceptional beauty, became the first Black woman featured on the cover of Life magazine, a white, mainstream publication. (B. 1922 – D. 1965). See *Actresses* to learn more about Dandridge.

OWEN/MASON FAMILY HOME

LATASHA COMPANY

MORTICIAN

▮ FIRST BLACK WOMAN TO OPEN FUNERAL CENTER IN LONG BEACH
▮ FIRST BLACK WOMAN PRESIDENT OF THE LOS ANGELES COUNTY FUNERAL DIRECTORS ASSOCIATION

In 2012, Latasha Company became the first Black woman to open her own funeral service business in the city of Long Beach. Over the years, she has made, and continues to make her mark in the mortician world. For example, Company was the first Black woman to serve as president of the Los Angeles County Funeral Directors Association and the first director to have her own crematorium. (B. Unknown).

MOTION PICTURE COMPANY

▮ FIRST MOTION PICTURE COMPANY CONTROLLED BY BLACKS IN THE UNITED STATES

In 1917, the Lincoln Motion Picture Company (LMPC) formed to produce films that depicted positive images of Black Americans. It was the first motion picture company controlled by Black people. LMPC's offices were located at 905 Central Avenue in South Los Angeles.

FILM REELS

HOMER L. GARROTT

MOTORCYCLE OFFICER

■ FIRST BLACK OFFICER HIRED BY THE CALIFORNIA HIGHWAY PATROL

Homer L. Garrott, the first Black patrolman in the history of the California Highway Patrol, was assigned to motorcycle duty for most of his 22 years with the CHP. Garrott attended law school when he was off duty and graduated from Southwestern University School of Law. He was admitted to the State Bar of California in 1960 and retired from the CHP four years later to work as a lawyer. Garrott worked as a deputy public defender from 1964 to 1967 and a juvenile court referee from 1967 to 1968.

He served as a Los Angeles Municipal Court commissioner from 1968 to 1973. In March 1973, then-Governor Ronald Reagan appointed him to the Compton Municipal Court. Garrott retired as a municipal cmn ourt judge in 1984, but he continued to serve as a part-time judicial officer. (B. 1915 – D. 1998). See *Highway Patrolman* to learn more about Garrott.

HIGHWAY PATROL
MOTORCYCLE

WILLIAM "BUDDY"
COLLETTE

HENRY LEWIS

MUSICIANS

▮ FIRST BLACK MUSICIAN APPOINTED TO A MAJOR SYMPHONY ORCHESTRA

Sixteen-year-old double bass player made history. When he was hired by the Los Angeles (LA) Philharmonic (Phil), Lewis became the first Black instrumentalist to play in a major symphony orchestra and one of the youngest players in LA Philharmonic history. In 1961, Lewis was appointed assistant conductor of LA Phil, a post he held from 1961 to 1965. In the process, he became the first Black conductor to lead a major orchestra on a regular season concert. In 1968, Lewis became the conductor and musical director of the New Jersey Symphony Orchestra, making him the first Black person to lead a major symphony orchestra in the United States. In 1972, Lewis became the first Black person to conduct at the Metropolitan Opera in New York City. When he died in 1996, his New York Times obituary dubbed him the Jackie Robinson of classical music. (B. 1932 – D. 1996).

▮ FIRST BLACK MUSICIAN IN A WEST COAST TELEVISION STUDIO BAND

A leading figure in the "bebop" and "cool jazz" movements, artist and musician William "Buddy" Collette was an important force in the LA jazz community. In 1949, Collette was the only African American member of the band for "You Bet Your Life", a radio show hosted by Groucho Marx. In 1951, Collette became the first Black musician in a west coast television studio band. (B. 1921 – D. 2010). See *Labor Leaders* for more information on Collette.

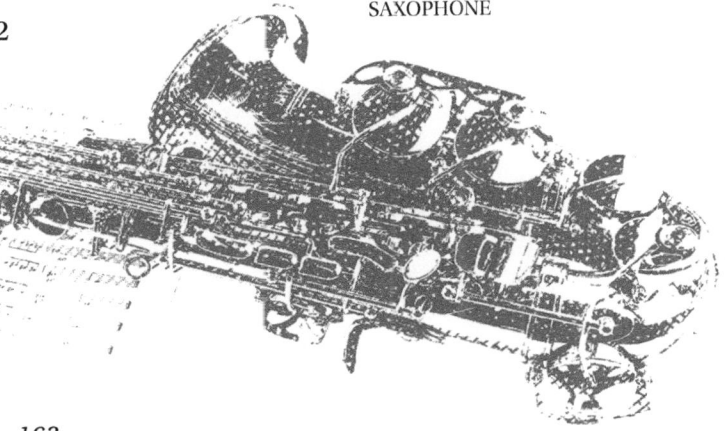

SAXOPHONE

CHAP

LOS ANGELES COUNTY HOSPITAL BUILDING, 1939

TER 14

FAY M. JACKSON

NEWSPAPER JOURNALIST

■ FIRST BLACK WOMAN TO BE NATIONALLY RENOWNED JOURNALIST

Fay M. Jackson, the first nationally renowned Black journalist, founded the first Black news magazine on the West Coast, *Flash*, in 1928 and, during the 1930s, worked for the Associated Negro Press (ANP) as their first credentialed Black Hollywood correspondent. In 1937, Jackson represented the ANP at the coronation of King George VI and interviewed Emperor Haile Selassie of Ethiopia.

As an ANP journalist, Jackson's work appeared in 75 Black American newspapers, 200 African newspapers, several magazines and on two radio stations. (B. 1902 – D. 1979). See *Hollywood Correspondent* to learn more about Jackson.

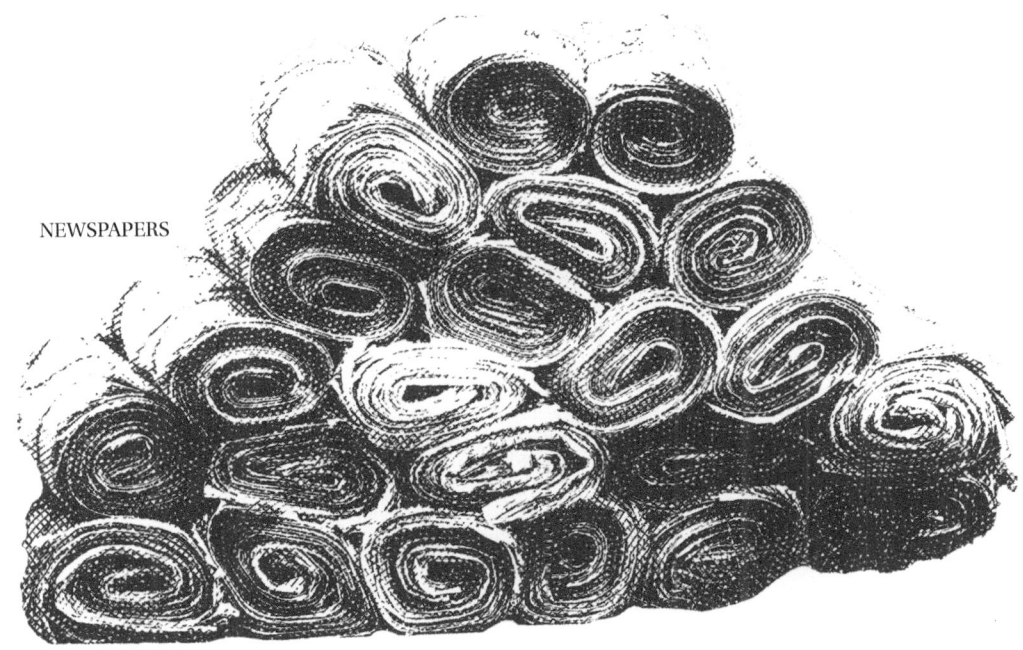

NEWSPAPERS

JOHN NEIMORE

NEWSPAPER OWNERS

FIRST BLACK NEWSPAPER IN LOS ANGELES

In 1879, John Neimore established the *California Owl* newspaper to help newly arrived Black people adapt to life in Los Angeles. The "Owl" contained information about housing, jobs and news items relevant to the Black community. In 1912, Neimore turned the Owl over to Charlotta Bass who renamed it "The California Eagle". (B. 1862 – D. 1912).

FIRST BLACK WOMAN NEWSPAPER OWNER/PUBLISHER

Multi-talented Charlotta Bass was a journalist, newspaper publisher/editor, community educator, civil rights activist, politician and owner of *The California Eagle* from 1912 to 1951. In 1912, John Neimore, founder of *The California Owl*, one of the first Black newspapers in California, appointed Bass as his successor and transferred ownership of T*he California Owl* to her. Bass renamed it *The California Eagle* and ran it for the next 40 years. At its height, the "Eagle", with a circulation of 60,000, was the largest Black newspaper on the West Coast. (B. 1874 – D. 1969).

CALIFORNIA EAGLE
NEWSPAPER

BETTY SMITH WILLIAMS

NURSES

■ FIRST BLACK PERSON TO RECEIVE NURSING SCHOOL CERTIFICATE FROM LOS ANGELES COUNTY GENERAL HOSPITAL NURSING SCHOOL

Late in 1919, Libbie Jennings Craft, a Los Angeles native who previously trained at the Lincoln School for Nurses in New York City, became the first Black person to receive a certificate from a Los Angeles (LA) County-run nursing school. Earlier in 1919, under the leadership of Dr. Charles Edward Block, the National Association for the Advancement of Colored People pressured the LA County Board of Supervisors to integrate the nursing school at LA County General Hospital. Block convinced the supervisors that Black students could have filled the desperate need for nurses during World War I, and saved lives, if they had been admitted. (B. Unknown – D. Unknown).

■ FIRST BLACK PUBLIC HEALTH PROFESSOR HIRED TO TEACH NURSING IN A CALIFORNIA UNIVERSITY

In 1956, Betty Smith Williams was hired to teach public health nursing at the University of California (UC), Los Angeles making her the first Black public health professor hired to teach in a California university and the first Black public health nursing professor in the UC system. In 1971, Williams co-founded the National Black Nurses Association and served as its president from 1995 to 1999. (B. Unknown – D. Unknown). See *Professor* for additional information about Williams.

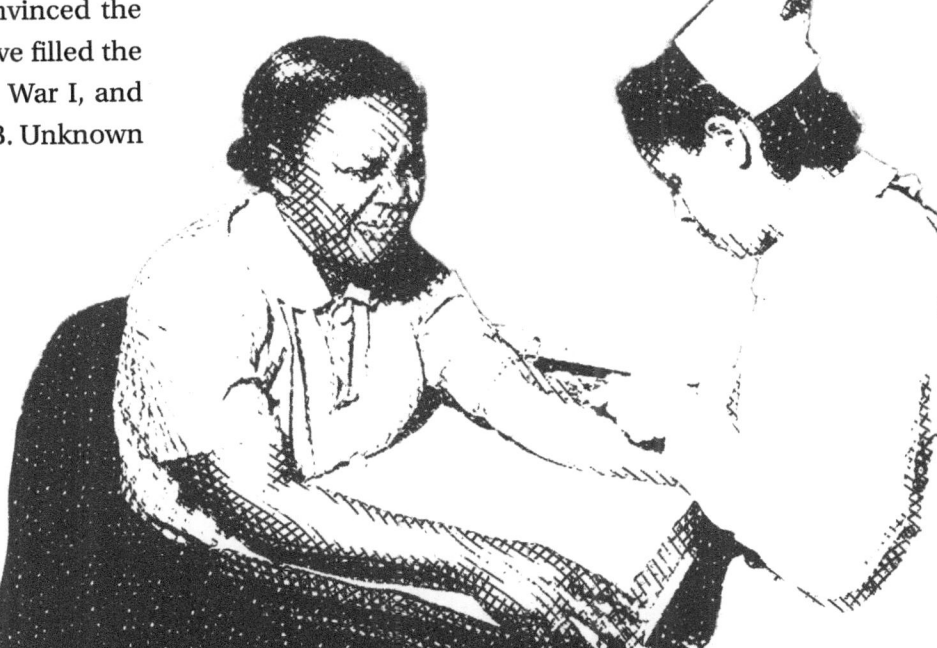

NURSE DRAWING BLOOD, 1941

CHAP

400 METER FINISH, 1984 OLYMPIC GAMES, LOS ANGELES MEMORIAL COLISEUM

VALERIE BRISCO-HOOKS

OLYMPIC STAR

■ FIRST OLYMPIAN TO WIN THE 200-METER AND 400-METER RACE IN THE SAME OLYMPICS (LA 84 OLYMPICS)

In the 1984 Olympic Games in Los Angeles (LA), South LA's home-grown track star, Valerie Brisco-Hooks, electrified the sports world when she won gold medals in 200 and 400-meter races in the same Olympic Games, accomplishing what no other athlete, man or woman, had ever done. She topped that off by adding another in the 4 x 400 meter relay. What makes her accomplishments even more amazing is that, Brisco-Hooks, who had given birth in 1982 and gained over forty pounds during her pregnancy, was the mother of a two-year-old. In 1995, she was inducted into the United States Track and Field Hall of Fame.

Her 400 meter time of 48.83, set while winning the 1984 Olympics was at the time the Olympic record and still ranks her as the tenth fastest woman of all time. Brisco-Hooks attended West Athens Elementary, Locke High School and California State University Northridge. (B. 1960).

LA MEMORIAL COLISEUM

175

CHAP

CENTRAL AVENUE POST OFFICE, EARLY 1900s

TER 16

VIVIAN STRANGE

GEORGIA ANN
ROBINSON

POLICE OFFICERS

■ FIRST BLACK POLICEMAN IN LOS ANGELES

In 1889, the Los Angeles Police Department hired Robert William Stewart, a formerly enslaved man, making him the city's first Black patrolman. He worked at the LAPD until May of 1900, when he was accused by a white teenager of sexual assault, and arrested. While he was awaiting trial, the police commission voted to fire him. A trial jury later heard the sexual assault charges, and acquitted him. In 2021, 90 years after Stewart's death, the Los Angeles Police Commission voted to posthumously reinstate him. In a statement, the commission said that Stewart had been "unjustly fired". (B. 1850 – D. 1931).

■ FIRST BLACK FEMALE POLICE OFFICER IN LOS ANGELES

In 1919, Georgia Ann Robinson, after having previously joined the LAPD as a volunteer in 1916, became the first Black woman to be appointed a police officer in Los Angeles. There were strict requirements for becoming a policewoman, such as being between age 30–44, being married, and holding a degree in education or nursing. Robinson was thirty-six years old, married, and had a degree in nursing, so she met all these requirements. She was officially sworn in on June 10, 1919. Officer Robinson worked on juvenile and homicide cases, including referring women and girls to social agencies, inspiring her to found the Sojourner Truth Home, a shelter for women and girls. Robinson's police career ended at the age of 49 when she permanently lost her sight after being injured by a prisoner. When asked, she said "I have no regrets. I didn't need my eyes any longer. I had seen all there was to see." After retiring, Robinson continued her community activism, working with the NAACP, volunteering in shelters, and campaigning to desegregate schools and beaches. (B. 1879 – D. 1961).

■ FIRST BLACK POLICE OFFICER TO DIE IN THE LINE OF DUTY

Officer Charles P. Williams was the first Black cop killed in the line of duty in Los Angeles. Williams, a 35-year-old vice squad officer, was gunned down Jan. 13, 1923, while responding to a report of an armed man threatening people. He and his partner were working undercover when they were flagged down by a citizen who told them a man was waving a gun at a nearby house. The officers knew this house to be a brothel. It was later discovered that the man was the landlord of the house and had entered to impose a vigilante clean-up of the house by evicting prostitutes. As they were driving there, the police car broke down and Policeman Williams decided to walk the rest of the way. Upon his arrival, he told the man to put his hands up. The suspect fired twice, striking Policeman Williams in the abdomen. A passing truck transported Policeman Williams to a nearby hospital where he died from his wounds. The suspect was later captured, but it is unknown what happened to him. The suspect claimed he did not know Policeman Williams was an officer. (B. 1888 – D. 1923).

■ FIRST BLACK FEMALE SERGEANT IN LOS ANGELES POLICE DEPARTMENT

In 1950, Vivian Strange Vivian Strange became the first Black woman promoted to the rank of sergeant in the LAPD. Strange, who had been a member of the force since 1942, had a complicated relationship with other officers, and because of their prejudicial treatment, refused to ride in the same car with many white officers when driving in South Los Angeles. Strange opted to drive herself, saying that "Black women who rode in cars with white men were likely to be seen as prostitutes which would undermine her authority and respect in the eyes of the community." (B. Unknown – D. Unknown).

■ FIRST BLACK CHIEF OF POLICE OF LOS ANGELES POLICE DEPARTMENT

On April 16, 1992, in a historic step designed to propel the Los Angeles (LA) Police Department on a course of sweeping reforms, the city Police Commission selected Philadelphia Police Commissioner Willie L. Williams to succeed embattled Chief Daryl F. Gates as the department's top official. The decision by LA Mayor Tom Bradley and LA Police Commission members made Williams the Police Department's first Black chief and the first outsider to assume command of the insular force in more than 40 years. (B. 1943 – D. 2016).

■ FIRST BLACK WOMAN PROMOTED TO CAPTAIN IN THE LOS ANGELES POLICE DEPARTMENT

In the year 2000, nineteen-year Los Angeles Police Department veteran Ann Young was appointed captain, making her the highest-ranking Black woman in the department's 131-year history. Of her experience within the police department Young said "This has been a road. There haven't always been open doors. Sometimes you take assignments you don't like because you want to stay on that road. You think about suing because things don't seem right. Then there's another way to go and you decide to take it instead." (B. Unknown).

▌ FIRST BLACK WOMAN PROMOTED TO COMMANDER IN THE LOS ANGELES POLICE DEPARTMENT

In June 2011, Regina Scott became the first Black woman appointed to the rank of commander in the Los Angeles Police Department. Scott was assigned as the assistant commanding officer of the Information Technology Bureau. (B. Unknown).

▌ FIRST BLACK WOMAN PROMOTED TO DEPUTY CHIEF IN THE LOS ANGELES POLICE DEPARTMENT

On July 12, 2018, longtime Los Angeles Police Department officer Regina Scott was promoted to deputy chief within the department. Scott made history as the first Black female officer to hold the high ranking position.

WILLIE L. WILLIAMS

JOHN A. SOMERVILLE

POLICE OVERSEERS

■ FIRST BLACK PERSON APPOINTED TO LOS ANGELES POLICE COMMISSION

In 1949, John A. Somerville, the first Black graduate and Doctor of Dentistry at the University of Southern California School of Dentistry, became the first Black person appointed to the Los Angeles Police Commission. (B. 1882 – D. 1972). See *Dental School Graduates* to learn more about Somerville.

■ FIRST BLACK WOMAN APPOINTED TO LOS ANGELES POLICE COMMISSION

In 1971, Marguerite Justice became the first Black woman, and the second Black person, to serve as a police commissioner, not only in Los Angeles, but in the entire United States. The *LA Times* asked Justice how she would respond to law-and-order problems in minority communities, Justice answered: "I'm Black. Therefore my sensitivities already extend to minorities. I'm not rich and so my sensitivities also extend to the poor and oppressed." (B. 1921 – D. 2009).

■ FIRST BLACK PRESIDENT OF THE BOARD OF POLICE COMMISSIONERS OF THE LOS ANGELES POLICE DEPARTMENT

July 29, 2003, in a unanimous vote, David S. Cunningham, III was elected president of the five-member LA Board of Police Commissioners. Cunningham graduated with his B.A. degree in Economics from the University of Southern California (USC) in 1977 and a Juris Doctor from the new York university School of Law in 1980. In 2009, Cunningham was appointed judge by then-Governor Arnold Schwarzeneggar and assigned to the Los Angeles Superior Court where he currently serves. Cunningham is the son of David S. Cunningham Jr., a Los Angeles City Council member from 1973 to 1987. (B. Unknown).

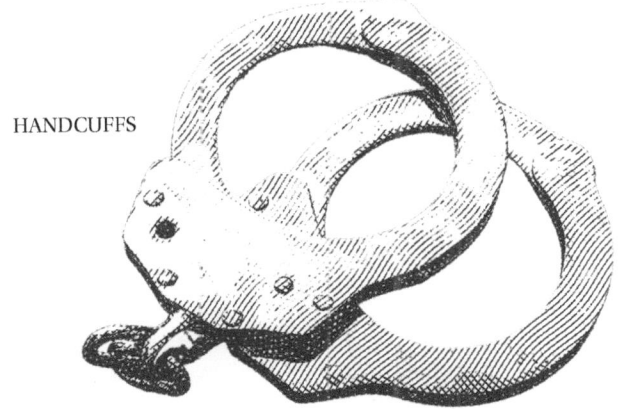

HANDCUFFS

NANCY C. AVERY

POSTMASTERS

▮ FIRST BLACK PERSON TO HEAD A POST OFFICE IN LOS ANGELES COUNTY

Nancy C. Avery was the first Black person to head a Post Office in Los Angeles County. Mrs. Avery, an active Democratic Party worker, was a housewife and school recreation assistant in 1961 when then-President John F. Kennedy named her postmaster of Pacoima. "The Democratic Party wanted to do something that had never been done before," she said just before retiring. "I was the token." Before her appointment, Postal Service officials said, the only other Black postmasters had worked in small rural post offices. After her retirement, she served as a commissioner and president of the Los Angeles Department of Animal Regulation. (B. 1920 – D. 1992).

▮ FIRST BLACK POSTMASTER GENERAL OF LOS ANGELES

In 1963, then-President John F. Kennedy appointed Leslie N. Shaw to the position of Postmaster General of Los Angeles (LA) of the third largest post office in the United States, making him the first Black person appointed to the position of postmaster for a major American city. (B. 1922 – D. 1985).

MAILBOX

SAMUEL B. MARLOWE

PRIVATE INVESTIGATOR

■ FIRST BLACK PRIVATE INVESTIGATOR IN LOS ANGELES

In the mid-1920s, private investigator Samuel B. Marlowe established his practice. Marlowe was born in Montego Bay, Jamaica and, according to his *Los Angeles Times* obituary, he served in Britain's Egyptian Expeditionary Force, a World War I fighting brigade that guarded the Suez Canal. After the war, Marlowe immigrated to the U.S., settling in Los Angeles, became a licensed investigator and opened a private detective agency. (B. 1890 – D. 1991).

PROFESSOR

■ FIRST BLACK PROFESSOR IN CALIFORNIA

In 1956, UCLA hired Betty Smith Williams to teach public health nursing making her the first Black person to teach at the university level in California. In 1971, Williams co-founded the National Black Nurses Association. It should be noted that, in 1933, Dr. Ruth Temple held a teaching position at White Memorial Hospital. (B. Unknown – D. Unknown). See *Nurses* to learn more about Williams. See *Doctors* and *Medical School Faculty* to learn more about Temple.

FOUNTAIN PEN AND BOUND LETTERS

BRIDGET "BIDDY"
MASON

PROPERTY OWNERS

■ FIRST BLACK WOMAN TO OWN PROPERTY IN LOS ANGELES

While Biddy Mason may not have been the very first, it's important to note that in 1866, Mason became one of the first Black women in Los Angeles to purchase property. (B. 1818 – D. 1891). See *Midwife* and *School* for more information about Mason.

■ FIRST BLACK FAMILY TO HAVE WRONGFULLY TAKEN LAND RETURNED

On July 7, 2022, dozens of people gathered on the oceanfront property known as Bruce's Beach to mark the first time the government ever returned land that had been wrongfully taken from a Black family. "Today, we're sending a message to every government in this nation confronted with the same challenge: This work is no longer unprecedented," said Los Angeles County Supervisor Janice Hahn, who had launched the complex legislative and legal process to transfer the property. "We have set the precedent, and it is the pursuit of justice."

BUILDINGS OWNED
BY BIDDY MASON

GERALDINE BURTON
BRANCH

PUBLIC HEALTH SCHOOL GRADUATE

▮ FIRST BLACK PERSON TO GRADUATE FROM UCLA SCHOOL OF PUBLIC HEALTH

Dr. Geraldine Burton Branch was a Black American obstetrician-gynecologist who practiced in New York City, NY and Los Angeles, CA. She received her B.S. from Hunter College in chemistry and physics in 1932 and her M.D. from New York Medical College in 1936. Dr. Branch was one of the first Black female physicians with a Doctor of Medicine degree (MD) to practice in Los Angeles.

In 1962, Dr. Branch received a master's degree in public health from the UCLA School of Public Health. It is highly likely that she was UCLA's first Black public health graduate. (B. 1908 – D. 2016).

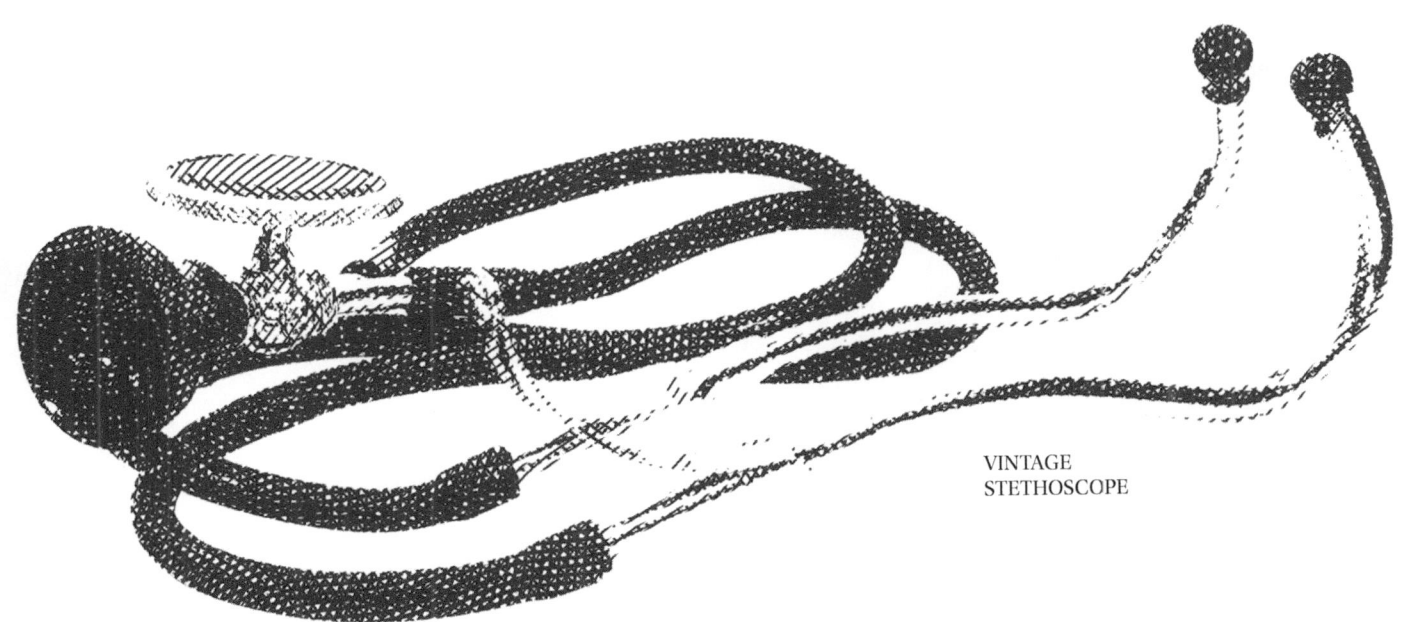

VINTAGE
STETHOSCOPE

191

USC vs. OREGON, 2012

WILLIAM VERNELL
WOOD SR.

QUARTERBACKS

■ FIRST BLACK COLLEGE QUARTERBACK IN LOS ANGELES

In 1957, William Vernell Wood Sr. played college football for the University of Southern California Trojans, becoming the first Black quarterback to play in what was the Pac-12 conference. In 1967, Wood was the starting free safety for the Green Bay Packers in Super Bowl I against the Kansas City Chiefs and Super Bowl II against the Oakland Raiders. Wood retired as a player after the 1971 season and was inducted into the Pro Football Hall of Fame in 1989. (B. 1936 – D. 2020).

■ FIRST BLACK PRO QUARTERBACK IN LOS ANGELES

In 1974, James "Shack" Harris became the first Black person to play quarterback for the Los Angeles Rams. That year, Harris led the Rams to their first playoff win in 23 years and became the first African American to start and win a playoff game in the NFL. During that 1974 season, Harris was named to the Pro Bowl and became the first Black quarterback to start and be named the game's Most Valuable Player. In 1975, Harris became the first Black quarterback to start in a NFL season opening game. (B. 1977).

JAMES "SHACK" HARRIS

QUILTERS

■ FIRST BLACK QUILTERS GUILD IN LOS ANGELES

Founded in the late 1980s, the African American Quilters of Los Angeles (AAQLA) first came together after an exhibit of African American quilts by Black quiltmakers held in the California African American Museum in Exposition Park of Los Angeles.

SEWING MACHINE

CHAP

LAFAYETTE SQUARE, LOS ANGELES, 1940

A.C. BILBREW

RADIO PERSONALITIES

■ FIRST BLACK SOLOIST ON RADIO IN LOS ANGELES

In 1923, A.C. Bilbrew, a leading figure in choral and gospel music, became the first Black soloist on radio in Los Angeles. (B. 1891 – D. 1972).

■ FIRST BLACK RADIO HOST IN LOS ANGELES

In 1942, poet, vocalist and businesswoman, A.C. Bilbrew became the first Black person to host a radio program in Los Angeles.

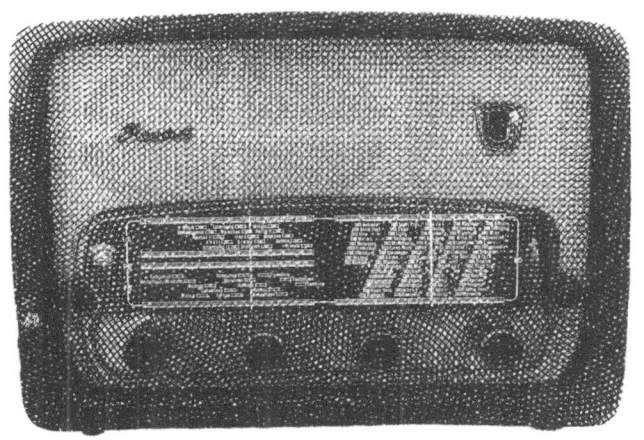

VINTAGE RADIO

■ FIRST VOICE OF BLACK LOS ANGELES

Nathaniel "The Magnificent Montague", one of the all-time baddest Los Angeles DeeJays, was notable not only for "Burn, Baby! Burn!", the rallying cry of the '65 Watts riots which rioters in Watts, California began shouting in response to housing discrimination, job discrimination and police brutality, he was also known for the soul music he promoted on LA's KGFJ radio station. Montague's popular catchphrase was referenced in the Apollo 11 software code that took America to the moon, as the Burn Baby Burn master ignition routine. (B. 1928).

■ FIRST BLACK SPORTS BROADCASTER IN LOS ANGELES

Brad Pye Jr., the first Black sports broadcaster in Los Angeles, served as sports director for four Black radio stations (KGFJ, KJLH, KACE and KDAY) for 21 years; and, sports editor of the *Los Angeles Sentinel* newspaper in the city for three decades. (B. 1931 – D. 2020).

TAVIS SMILEY

RADIO STATIONS

■ FIRST LOS ANGELES RADIO STATION TO FOCUS ON BLACK COMMUNITY

In 1959, radio station KGFJ became the first radio station in Los Angeles, and one of the first in the U.S., to focus its broadcasting towards the Black community.

■ FIRST BLACK-OWNED RADIO STATION IN LOS ANGELES

KJLH is LA's oldest continuously Black-owned radio station (and perhaps the oldest on the West Coast). Here's the backstory. In 1965, Black businessman John Lamar Hill, then owner of the Angelus Funeral Home based in South Los Angeles, bought a radio station and, using his initials as the call letters, relaunched it as KJLH with a Black radio format. In 1979, Hill sold KJLH to musician Stevie Wonder. (B. 1923 – D. 1998).

■ FIRST HIP-HOP RADIO STATION IN LOS ANGELES

On September 16, 1979, KDAY 1580-AM disc jockey Steve Woods played The Sugarhill Gang's "Rapper's Delight" essentially creating LA's first hip-hop radio station.

■ FIRST BLACK-OWNED TALK RADIO STATION IN LOS ANGELES

In 2020, former BET, PBS and NPR/Public Radio International host Tavis Smiley's Smiley Radio Properties purchased 1580 KBLA for $7.15 million. On June 19, 2021, KBLA Talk 1580, helmed by Tavis Smiley, went live making it the only Black-owned and operated talk station in Los Angeles, California. (B. 1964).

PORTABLE STEREO / BOOMBOX

HARRIET
OWENS-BYNUM

REAL ESTATE MOGUL

■ FIRST WOMAN OF ANY RACE/ETHNICITY TO RUN LARGE-SCALE REAL ESTATE SALES OPERATION

Harriet Owens-Bynum was the first woman of any race to manage a large-scale real estate operation in Los Angeles. In the 1890s, Owens-Bynum, and her family, bought and sold more than 65 houses and lots, and rented properties to Black families in Boyle Heights and other areas of the city. (B. Unknown – D. 1933).

REAL ESTATE ORGANIZATION

■ FIRST BLACK REAL ESTATE ORGANIZATION IN LOS ANGELES

In 1949, in response to racism, discrimination and redlining, Black real estate professionals in Los Angeles formed the Consolidated Realty Board of Southern California, calling its members "realtists" because the white group had patented the term "realtor." On March 16, 1950, the group received an official charter from the California Secretary of State. Their first office was located at Western Avenue and 36th Place. In 1973, they relocated to their present location on Don Felipe Drive in scenic Baldwin Hills. The group provides training for real estate professionals as well as homebuyers and advocates for fair housing legislation.

HOUSING DESIGNED BY
A BLACK ARCHITECT

THE SPIKES BROTHERS

RECORD COMPANY

■ FIRST BLACK-OWNED RECORD COMPANY

Sunshine Records, a small Los Angeles-based (LA) record label founded by the Spikes Brothers (John Spikes & Reb Spikes), owner/operators of a music store that catered to LA's Black community. In the early 1920s, Sunshine Records produced 6 double-sided gramophone records of early jazz and blues. One of their biggest artists was Kid Ory's Creole Jazz Band. John Spikes (B. 1881 – D. 1955). Reb Spikes (B. 1888 – D. 1982).

RESTAURANT OWNER

■ FIRST BLACK-OWNED RESTAURANT IN LOS ANGELES

Though early records are murky due to a lack of primary source historical records, according to historian Douglas Flamming, in *Bound for Freedom: Black Los Angeles in Jim Crow America*, in October 1888, an early Black paper called *The Weekly Observer* mentioned a Black man named Frank Blackburn's new "coffee and chop house" at 1st Street and Los Angeles Street.

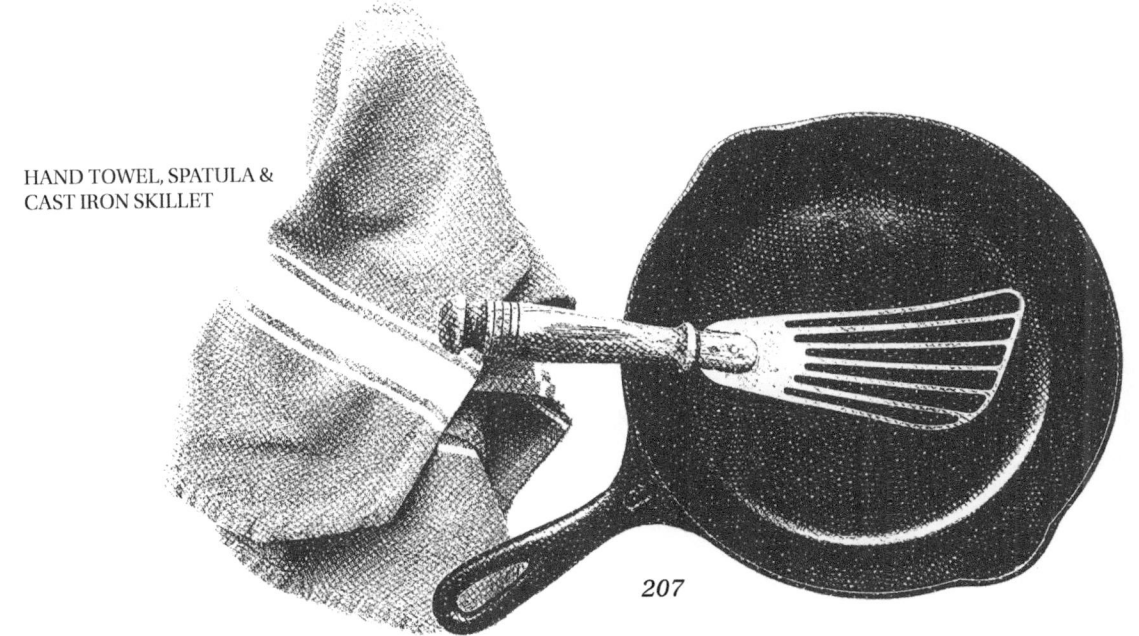

HAND TOWEL, SPATULA &
CAST IRON SKILLET

CHAP

SOUTH PASADENA HIGH SCHOOL, 1923

FAY E. ALLEN

SCHOOL

■ FIRST BLACK PRESCHOOL/EARLY CHILDHOOD EDUCATION CENTER

In 1866, pioneering philanthropist Biddy Mason, opened the city's first preschool/early childhood education center in her home. (B. 1818 – D. 1891). See *Midwife* and *Property Owners* to learn more about Mason.

■ FIRST ALL BLACK SCHOOL BUILT IN LOS ANGELES

The 51st Street School, constructed in 1910, was the first school in Los Angeles built in a Black community to accommodate students in a Black neighborhood known as the Furlong Tract. It was a one-story, wood-frame, four-room building with two brick posts that cost $8,720 and fronted 51st Street. When it opened, because of discriminatory hiring practices that kept Black teachers out of districts in many cities, the school hired white teachers and a white principal. However, the year after it was built, Bessie Burke became the schools' first Black teacher (1911) and the schools' first Black principal (1918). The original school building which burned down in 1922, was replaced and renamed Holmes Ave. Elementary School. In 1933, the new building suffered earthquake damage and was remodeled.

SCHOOL BOARD MEMBER

■ FIRST BLACK PERSON ELECTED TO LOS ANGELES SCHOOL BOARD

In 1939, Fay E. Allen became the first Black person elected to the Los Angeles public school board. Despite widespread support from the teacher's union and other labor organizations, Allen's tenure was subject to overwhelming scrutiny and blatant racism. A political column from May 8, 1939, commented on the election results in language that reflected the racial feelings of the period: "Town full of squawks because Mrs. Fay Allen, a Negro music teacher, was elected to the Board of Education. Said squawks should be silenced. No intelligent person should complain because he voted for Mrs. Allen, not knowing her race. Mrs. Allen is intelligent, traveled and experienced." (B. 1887 – D. 1974).

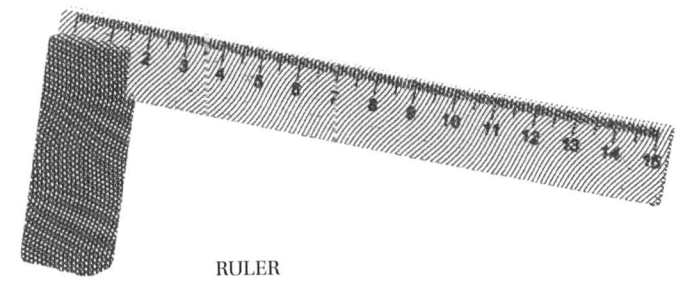

RULER

BESSIE BURKE

SCHOOL PRINCIPAL

■ FIRST BLACK PRINCIPAL IN THE LOS ANGELES PUBLIC SCHOOL SYSTEM

In 1918, when Bessie Burke was hired at the 51st Street School, now Holmes Elementary, she became the first Black principal in the Los Angeles public school system. See *School Teacher* to learn more about Burke. (B. 1891 – D. 1968).

■ FIRST BLACK PRINCIPAL TO HEAD RACIALLY INTEGRATED SCHOOL IN LOS ANGELES PUBLIC SCHOOL SYSTEM

In 1938, Bessie Burke became the first Black principal to head a racially integrated school (Nevin Avenue School) in the Los Angeles public school system.

SCHOOL DESK

MICHELLE KING

SCHOOL SUPERINTENDENT

SCHOOL TEACHER

▪ FIRST BLACK WOMAN APPOINTED SUPERINTENDENT OF THE LOS ANGELES PUBLIC SCHOOL SYSTEM

On January 11, 2016, Dr. Michelle King became the Los Angeles Unified School District's first female superintendent in 80 years and the first Black woman to serve as the LAUSD Superintendent. King spent her entire career in LAUSD, attending its schools and even working as a teacher's aide. When she was promoted to superintendent, she said, "I want to be a role model for students who look like me." In 2017, King was named the National Association of School Superintendents', Superintendent of the Year. King, a champion of unity and collaboration among all public schools, passed away at age 57 after fighting cancer. King said: "Sometimes in life, we don't think that certain positions are available to us particularly if you're a youth, a minority, that job or that position or that role might not be for you because you don't see many role models, you don't see many folks in those positions," King said. "I feel that the appointment has said to particularly young women that anything is possible." King, a graduate of UCLA, received her doctorate in Education from USC. (B. 1961 – D. 2019).

▪ FIRST BLACK TEACHER IN THE LOS ANGELES PUBLIC SCHOOL SYSTEM

In 1911, after graduating from the Los Angeles State Normal School (now UCLA), Bessie Burke received her teaching credentials and was hired by the Los Angeles Public School system, making Burke the first Black teacher in the district. Later, in 1918, she became the first Black principal in the system. After a 44-year career in education, Burke retired from the LA Board of Education in 1955. Burke is remembered as a distinguished humanitarian and well-respected educator and administrator. She served in a number of civic organizations including, the YWCA, Native California Club, the NAACP and Delta Sigma Theta Sorority, Inc. On March 17, 2009, Burke's home was included on the list of *Historic Resources Associated with African Americans in Los Angeles* and listed on the National Register of Historic Places. (B. 1891 – D. 1968). See *School Principal* to learn more about Burke.

JULIUS BOYD LOVING

SHERIFFS

◼ FIRST BLACK DEPUTY SHERIFF

Julius Boyd Loving was sworn in as a Los Angeles County deputy sheriff, making him LA County's first Black sheriff. An innovative administrator, Loving was the driving force behind the creation of the first jail store and for introducing the jail's inmate craft programs including the jail carpenter shop, shoe shop, and tailor shop. In addition, Loving founded the Prisoners' Art Exhibit which displayed paintings and other creative works produced by inmates. Loving retired in January 1937 after thirty-four years of service. (B. 1863 – D. 1938).

◼ FIRST BLACK PERSON PROMOTED TO CHIEF IN LOS ANGELES COUNTY SHERIFF'S DEPARTMENT

In 1995, Helena Ashby became the first Black person (and first female) promoted to the rank of chief in the Los Angeles County Sheriff's Department. (B. 1942).

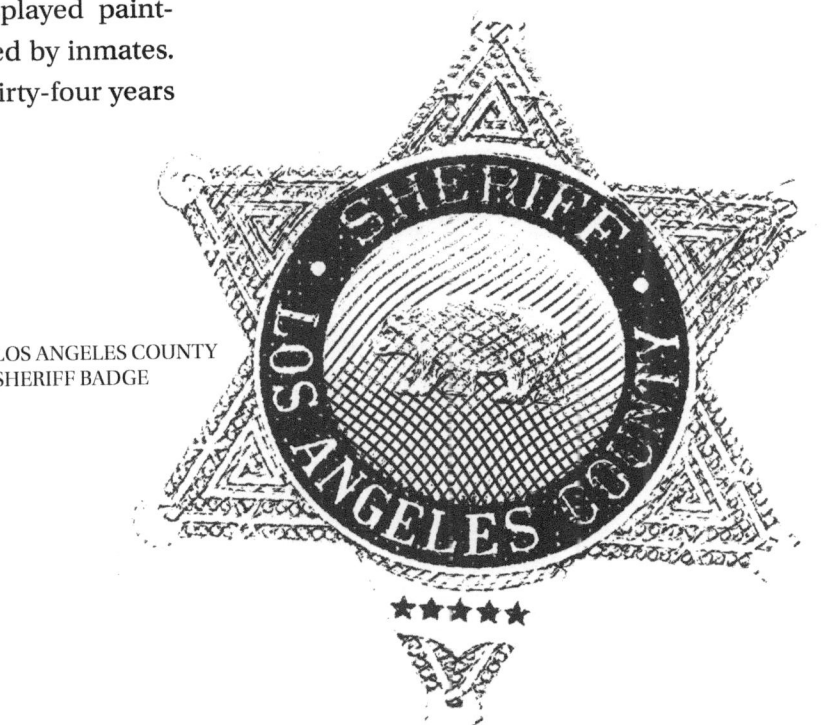

LOS ANGELES COUNTY
SHERIFF BADGE

COBI JONES

SOCCER STAR

■ FIRST BLACK SOCCER STAR OF LOS ANGELES

Cobi Jones, LA's first Black soccer star, grew up playing youth soccer in Los Angeles. He starred for the UCLA Bruins from 1988 to 1991, and, in 1990, won a national championship. He played for the U.S. Men's Soccer Team (USMNT) in the 1994, 1998, and 2002 FIFA World Cups. After starting his professional career in England, Jones joined the Major League Soccer's (MLS) Los Angeles (LA) Galaxy soccer team in 1996. In 1998, Jones was named U.S. Soccer Athlete of the Year. With the LA Galaxy, Jones won MLS championships in 2002 and 2005 as well as the U.S. Open Cup in 2001 and 2005 and the CONCACAF Champions Cup in 2000. From 1996 through 2007, as a player, and then, from 2008 to 2010, as interim head coach, Jones, LA's "original Cobi", spent 15 seasons with the Galaxy. From winning a national championship at UCLA, scoring the first goal in LA Galaxy history, being named athlete of the year, winning a national championship, winning professional championships, being the all-time leader in appearances for the USMNT, to maintaining the title of the longest standing member of the, at that time, MLS dynasty LA Galaxy, Jones had a stellar soccer career. In June 2011, Jones was inducted into the National Soccer Hall of Fame. (B. 1970).

STREET RACING

■ FIRST BLACK-LED STREET RACING ASSOCIATION

In 1965, Big Willie Robinson, the undisputed King of LA street racing, founded the Brotherhood of Street Racers, a group that, starting in the late '60s pushed a message that men and women working on engines and racing cars could bring peace to an LA torn apart by the Watts riots. Beginning in the mid-1970s, Willie ran a drag strip, Brotherhood Raceway Park (BRP), on Terminal Island in the Port of Los Angeles. BRP closed in 1995. (B. 1942 – D. 2012).

SOCCER BALL

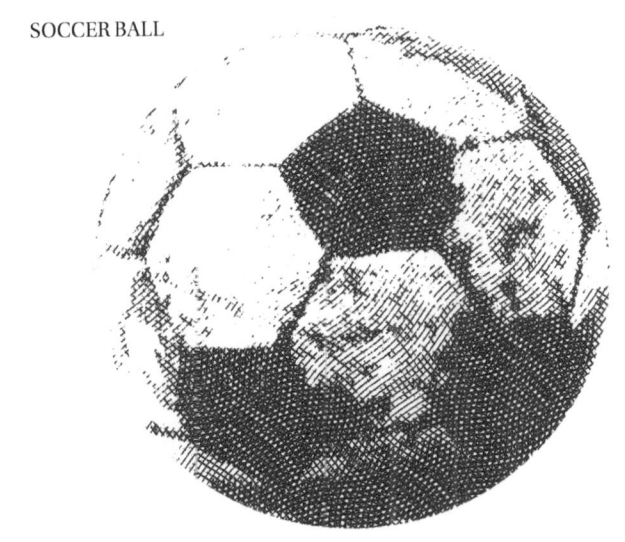

NICOLÁS ROLANDO
GABALDÓN

SURFERS

■ FIRST BLACK (AFRO-MEXICAN) SURFER

In 1951 Nicolás Rolando Gabaldón was recognized as the first documented Black surfer in LA. Gabaldón taught himself how to surf at the Negro Beach in Santa Monica—aka "the Inkwell"—the only beach in Southern California that racial minorities were freely allowed to use without harassment or violence. Gabaldón died on June 6, 1951 after his surfboard crashed into the Malibu Pier. (B. 1927 – D. 1951).

■ FIRST BLACK SURFING CHAMPION

In 1981, at age 12, Los Angeles-native Solo Scott won both the West Coast and U.S. amateur surfing championships making him the first Black surfing champion in the world. (B. 1982).

■ FIRST BLACK SURFING DIRECTOR

In 1982, David Lansdowne, a skilled Black surfer, became regional director of the Western Surfing Association (WSA). Later, he served as the first Black president of the WSA (1982–1992). (B. mid-1950s).

■ FIRST BLACK FEMALE PROFESSIONAL SURFER

In 1998, Sharon Schaffer, became the first Black woman to compete on a professional surfing tour. Schaffer said, "It's just been a battle to survive, all of it, all of the time, just for the right to be...". In referring to the racism she's experienced in her life both in and out of the water, "I had to develop a voice right away to scream: 'I got it — it's mine, my wave. I have a right to be on this wave.'" (B. Unknown).

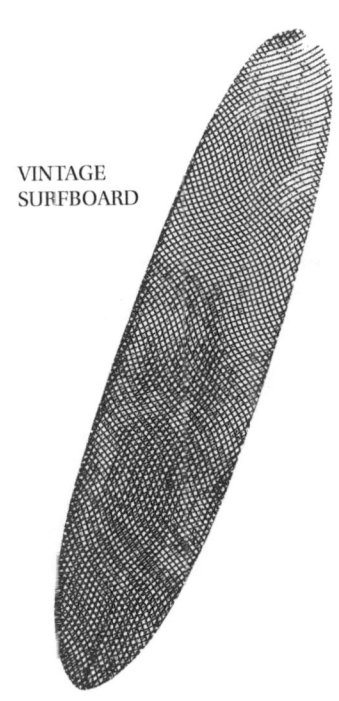

VINTAGE
SURFBOARD

CHAP

VIEW OF HOLLYWOOD, 1968

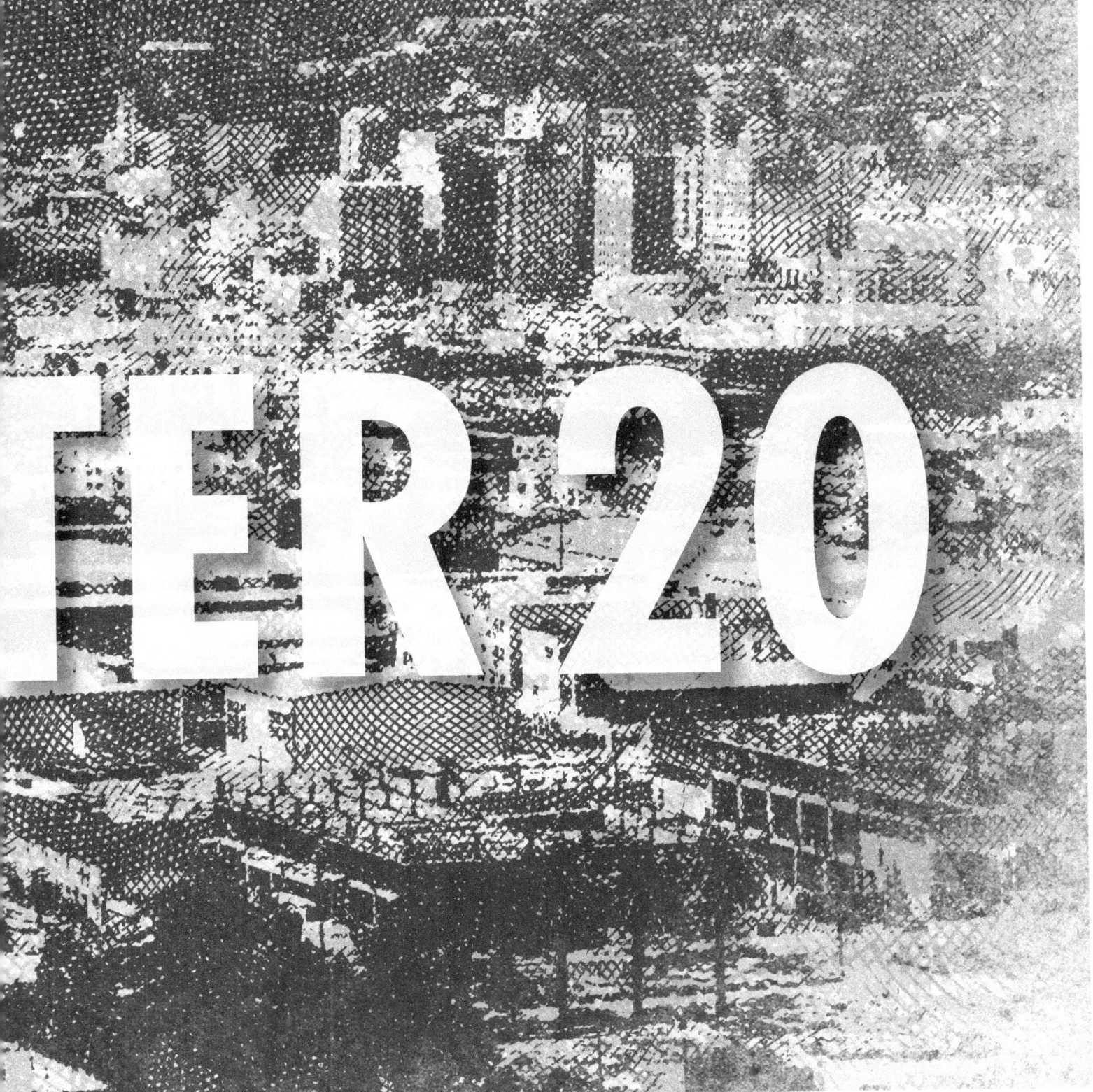

WALLACE "WALLY"
AMOS

TALENT AGENT

■ FIRST BLACK HOLLYWOOD TALENT AGENT AT WHITE TALENT AGENCY

In 1962, Wallace "Wally" Amos, later "Famous Amos", was hired as the first Black agent at William Morris making him the first Black talent agent at a major firm. Amos signed Simon & Garfunkel and headed the agency's rock 'n' roll department, attracting clients by sending them chocolate chip cookies along with an invitation to visit him. Amos represented musicians such as The Temptations, Sam Cooke, and Marvin Gaye. "He worked with all the Motown acts, with the Temptations and Supremes," his son, musician Shawn Amos said.

By 1967, Amos, after facing difficulties signing major acts to exclusive contracts, decided to strike out on his own saying "I never had a superstar but I made a day-to-day living, that was about it". Around 1973, after noting the popularity of his cookies, Amos decided to combine his salesmanship and baking abilities, gained the backing of major artists like Marvin Gaye, transformed himself into Wally "Famous" Amos and created a cookie empire. (B. 1936). See *Cookie King* to learn more about Amos.

THE TEMPTATIONS

NAT KING
COLE

HADDA
BROOKS

TELEVISION SHOW HOSTS

■ FIRST BLACK TELEVISION SHOW HOST IN LOS ANGELES

In 1956, Nat King Cole's eponymous television show, The Nat King Cole Show, made him the first Black television show host in Los Angeles. Cole's show was not the first national television program in the United States hosted by a Black person, Hazel Scott (in 1950) and Billy Daniels (in 1952) had each starred in short-lived and quickly forgotten variety shows, however Cole's program was the first hosted by a star of his magnitude. (B. 1919 – D. 1965).

■ FIRST BLACK WOMAN TO HOST HER OWN TV SHOW IN THE UNITED STATES

In 1957, Hadda Brooks, best known as the Queen of the Boogie, became the first Black Woman in the entire United States of America to host her own television show. *The Hadda Brooks Show*, a combination talk and musical entertainment show, aired on Los Angeles' television station KCOP. The show opened with Brooks seated behind a grand piano, cigarette smoke curling about her. She appeared in 26 half-hour episodes of the show. In 1993, Brooks was inducted in the Rhythm and Blues Foundation Hall of Fame. In 2007, a 72-minute documentary on Brooks's life, Queen of the Boogie, directed by Austin Young and Barry Pett, was presented at the Los Angeles Silver Lake Film Festival. (B. 1916 – D. 2002).

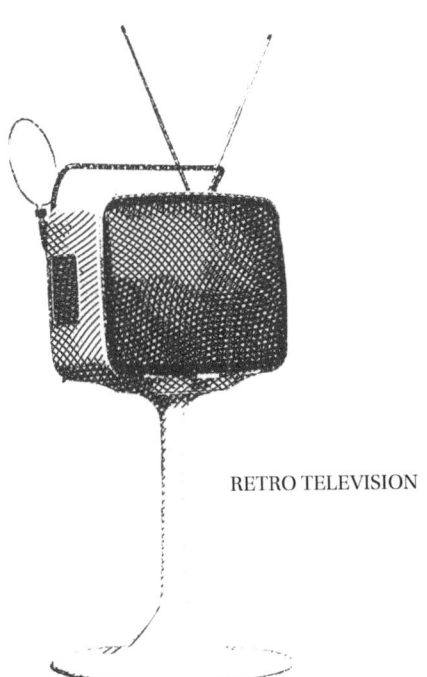

RETRO TELEVISION

KEN JONES

TELEVISION NEWS ANCHORMAN

▮ FIRST BLACK TELEVISION NEWS ANCHORMAN

Ken Jones, Los Angeles' first Black television anchorman, took over the daily anchor's chair on KTTV Channel 11 in 1972. Determined to serve the Black community as well as make his mark in mainstream journalism, Jones created the Black entertainment newsmagazine *SOUL* in 1966 and published it until 1982. He also founded the weekly Black newspaper the *Los Angeles Spirit* in late 1978, but that folded in less than a year. Born and raised in Los Angeles (LA), Jones began reporting high school sports for the *Los Angeles Herald Examiner* in 1954. He worked as a copy boy, jazz disc jockey and LA Police Department radio dispatcher while attending night school at LA City College. Jones worked for KDAY radio and KRLA radio in Pasadena before moving to KTTV as a features reporter and weekend anchor in 1968. (B. 1938 – D. 1993).

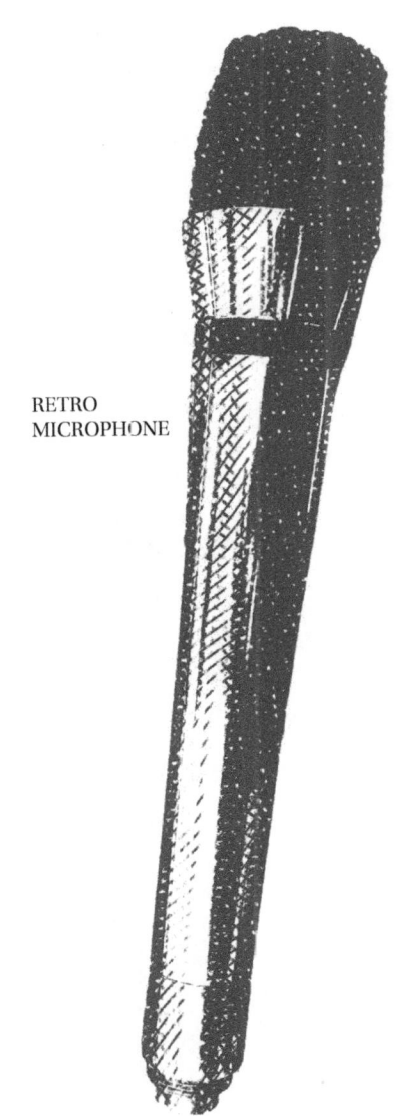

RETRO MICROPHONE

STEPHANIE WIGGINS

TRANSPORTATION EXPERTS

■ FIRST WOMAN CHIEF OF LOS ANGELES COUNTY METROLINK SYSTEM

On December 14, 2018, the Metrolink Board of Directors hired Stephanie Wiggins to direct the agency, making her the first woman and the first Black person to hold the position in Metrolink's (Southern California's commuter rail agency) 26-year history. (B. Unknown).

■ FIRST BLACK WOMAN NAMED CHIEF OF LOS ANGELES METRO AUTHORITY

On April 8, 2021, the Board of Directors of the Los Angeles County Metropolitan Transportation Authority voted to appoint Stephanie Wiggins to the position of chief executive officer. Wiggins was the first woman, and first Black woman, to serve in this role.

■ FIRST BLACK BUS OPERATOR IN LOS ANGELES

See *Bus Driver* for more information.

■ FIRST BLACK OFFICER HIRED BY CALIFORNIA HIGHWAY PATROL

See *Highway Patrolman* for more information.

■ FIRST BLACK MOTORCYCLE OFFICER

See *Motorcycle Officer* for more information.

■ FIRST BLACK TRANSPORTATION ENGINEER IN LOS ANGELES

See *Engineers* for more information.

FREEWAY INTERCHANGE

CHAP

CALIFORNIA STATE NORMAL SCHOOL, 1885

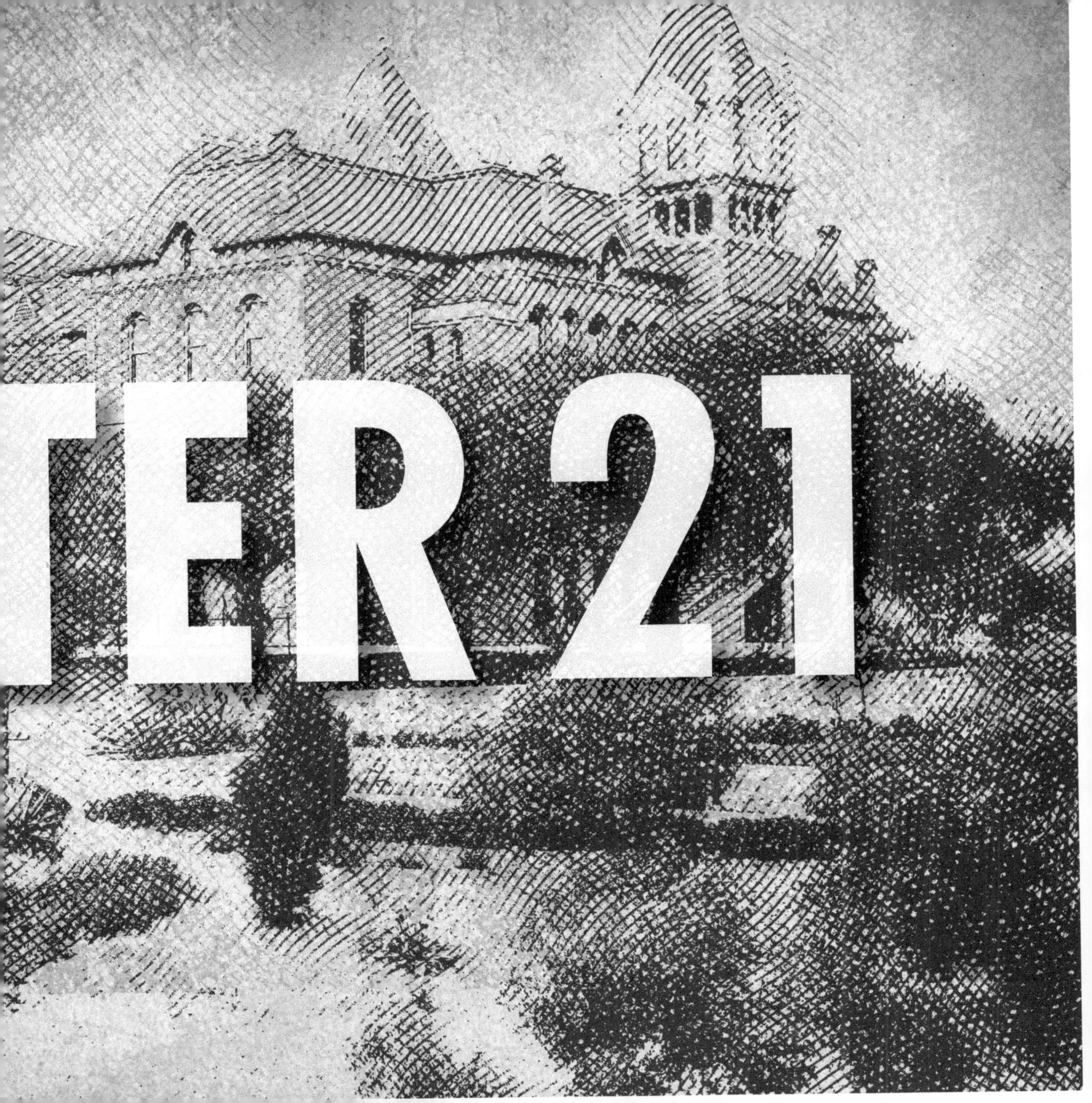
TER 21

DIANA MCNEIL PIERSON

ALICE ROWEN
JOHNSON

UNIVERSITY GRADUATES

▋ FIRST BLACK UCLA STUDENT
▋ FIRST BLACK UCLA GRADUATE

In 1888, at the age of 16 years old, Alice Rowen Johnson was the first Black person admitted into the State Normal School in Los Angeles (now the University of California, Los Angeles). In 1888, Johnson earned a degree in education making her the university's first Black graduate. (B. 1868 – D. 1912).

▋ FIRST BLACK WOMAN TO GRADUATE FROM USC

In 1894, Laura Gertrude Brown graduated with a degree in Music. (B. Unknown – D. Unknown).

▋ FIRST BLACK USC DOUBLE MAJOR

In 1909 Diana McNeil Pierson became the first Black woman to graduate from USC, receiving a B.A.'s in History and English. (B. Unknown – D. Unknown).

CALIFORNIA STATE
NORMAL SCHOOL

CHAP

LOS ANGELES FROM COURT HOUSE HILL, 1870

RALPH JOHNSON BUNCHE

VALEDICTORIANS

■ FIRST BLACK VALEDICTORIAN IN LOS ANGELES (UCLA)
■ FIRST BLACK NOBEL PRIZE RECIPIENT

Ralph Johnson Bunche was the first Black valedictorian in Los Angeles (LA). Bunche was the valedictorian of LA's Jefferson High School, attended UCLA, and, in 1927, graduated as the valedictorian of his class. In 1950, as a diplomat working for the United Nations, Bunche became the first Black person to receive the Nobel Peace Prize. Ebony magazine proclaimed him perhaps the most influential Black American of the first half of the 20th century and said that Bunche was the most celebrated Black American of his time. (B. 1904 – D. 1971).

■ FIRST BLACK VALEDICTORIAN AT UNIVERSITY OF SOUTHERN CALIFORNIA (USC)

In 2021, Tianna Shaw-Wakeman became USC's first Black valedictorian when she graduated with a master's degree student in social entrepreneurship from USC's Marshall School of Business. Shaw-Wakeman earned her bachelor's degree in psychology from USC's Dornsife College of Letters, Arts and Sciences. (B. Unknown).

ROYCE HALL, UCLA

JANE HINTON

PIONEERING BLACK
VETERINARIAN

VETERINARIAN

■ FIRST BLACK VETERINARIAN AT A MAJOR UNITED STATES ZOO

In September of 1972, Dr. Rosalie A. Reed became the first Black woman to work as a veterinarian at the LA Zoo and the first Black veterinarian employed at a major zoo in the United States. Reed, along with other LA zoo veterinarians, was responsible for the health, diet and general well-being of over 3,000 birds, reptiles and mammals. (B. 1945).

VOTER

■ FIRST BLACK REGISTERED VOTER

In 1870, after having been denied the right to register to vote by a Los Angeles County voter registrar, Lewis Gomez Green hired an attorney, sued the county in civil court, and lost. However, because the United States Congress had recently enacted laws that imposed fines and penalties on those who obstructed individuals from exercising their voting rights, the county recanted. On June 21, 1870, Green registered to vote along with two other Black men. See *Janitor* to learn more about Green. (B. 1827 – D. 1885).

BLACK VOTERS CASTING THEIR BALLOTS

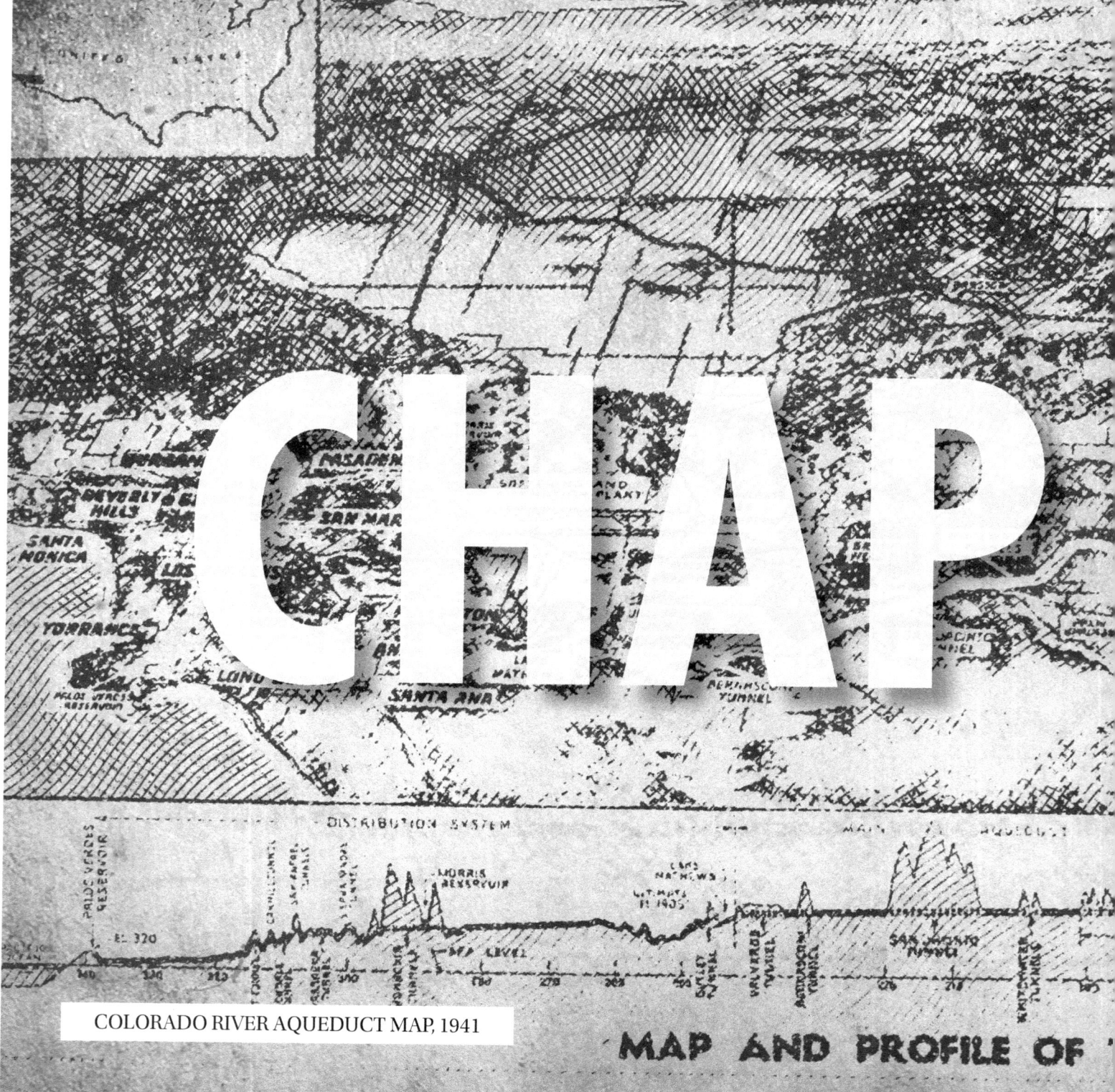

CHAP

COLORADO RIVER AQUEDUCT MAP, 1941

MAP AND PROFILE OF

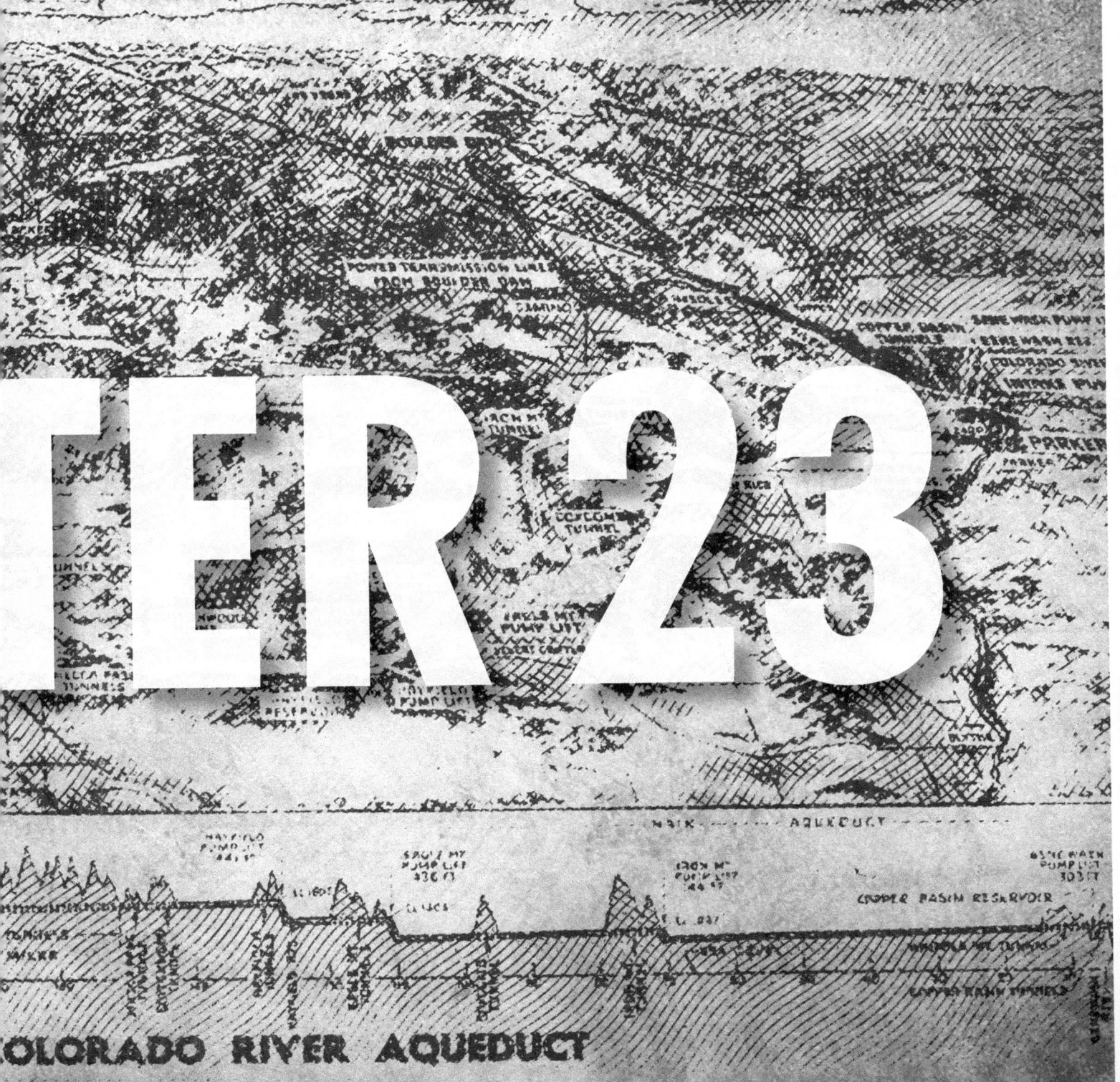

COLORADO RIVER AQUEDUCT

GLORIA D. GRAY

WATER BOARD CHAIRWOMAN

▮ FIRST BLACK PERSON TO SERVE AS CHAIR OF THE METROPOLITAN WATER DISTRICT

In 2019, the Metropolitan Water District of Southern California (MWD) Board of Directors elected Gloria D. Gray to serve as chairwoman of the MWD board. Gray is the first Black woman in Metropolitan's 90-year history to hold the position and the first person of any (nonwhite) race/ethnicity to become chair. MWD is the primary water importer and wholesaler for nearly 19 million people in six counties. In the November 2022 election, Gray simultaneously ran for West Basin Municipal Water District and the Inglewood City Council, ultimately winning both races. Despite concerns she may be violating a state law prohibiting elected officials from holding offices with overlapping responsibilities, Gray said "My intention is to serve my constituents in both capacities.

I'm focused on the issues in the city of Inglewood and I'm focused on the issues as it relates to West Basin." Gray earned her Bachelor of Science Degree in the Business Administration Program at the University of Redlands and her Health Services Management Certificate from the University of California Los Angeles. She earned a Louis Allen Management Certificate from the Los Angeles County Department of Health Services, where she spent her entire 36-year career. (B. Unknown).

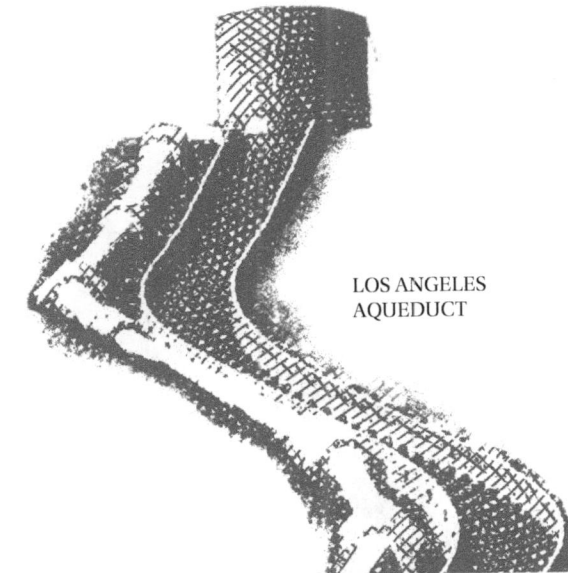

LOS ANGELES AQUEDUCT

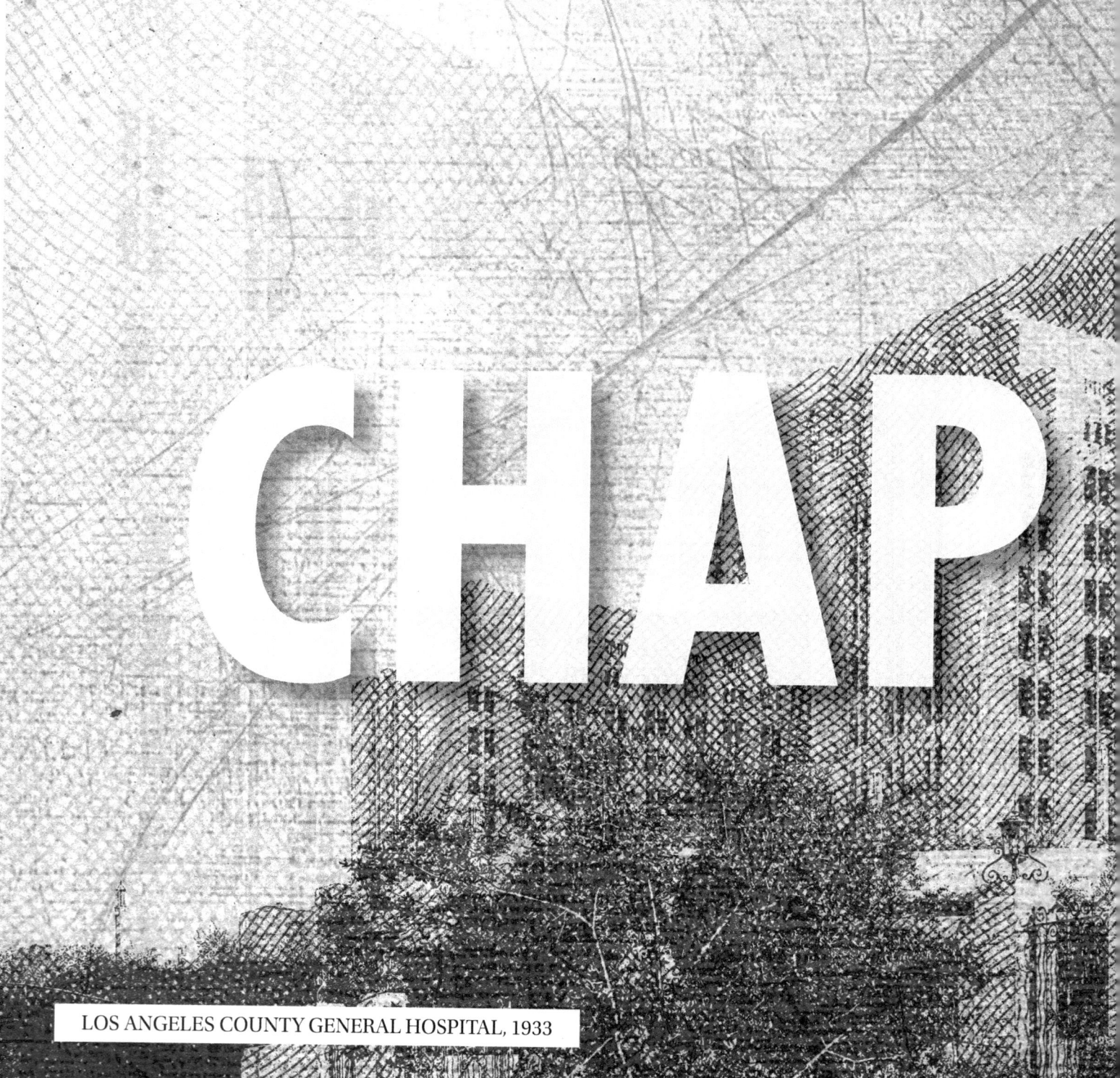

CHAP

LOS ANGELES COUNTY GENERAL HOSPITAL, 1933

TER 24

RALEIGH BLEDSOE

X-RAY SPECIALIST

■ FIRST BLACK RADIOLOGIST IN CALIFORNIA
■ FIRST BLACK RADIOLOGIST IN LOS ANGELES

In 1954, Dr. Raleigh Bledsoe became the first board-certified Black radiologist west of the Rockies. Bledsoe achieved academic and athletic success at Compton College, where he made the dean's list and established a national record for the Junior College broad jump, and the University of California, Los Angeles.

In 1944, while serving in the Army, Bledsoe earned his medical degree from Meharry Medical College in Tennessee. After interning at Los Angeles County General Hospital, Bledsoe served as a captain in the U.S. Army Medical Corps from 1945–48 and was a member of the Tuskegee Airmen. He later completed his residency in radiology at the University of Southern California. In 1952, he completed a residency in radiology at the University of Southern California. Bledsoe was the first Black doctor, and established the longest tenure as chief of service in the history of the organization (1954–1986).

VINTAGE X-RAY
MACHINE

CHAP

TER 25

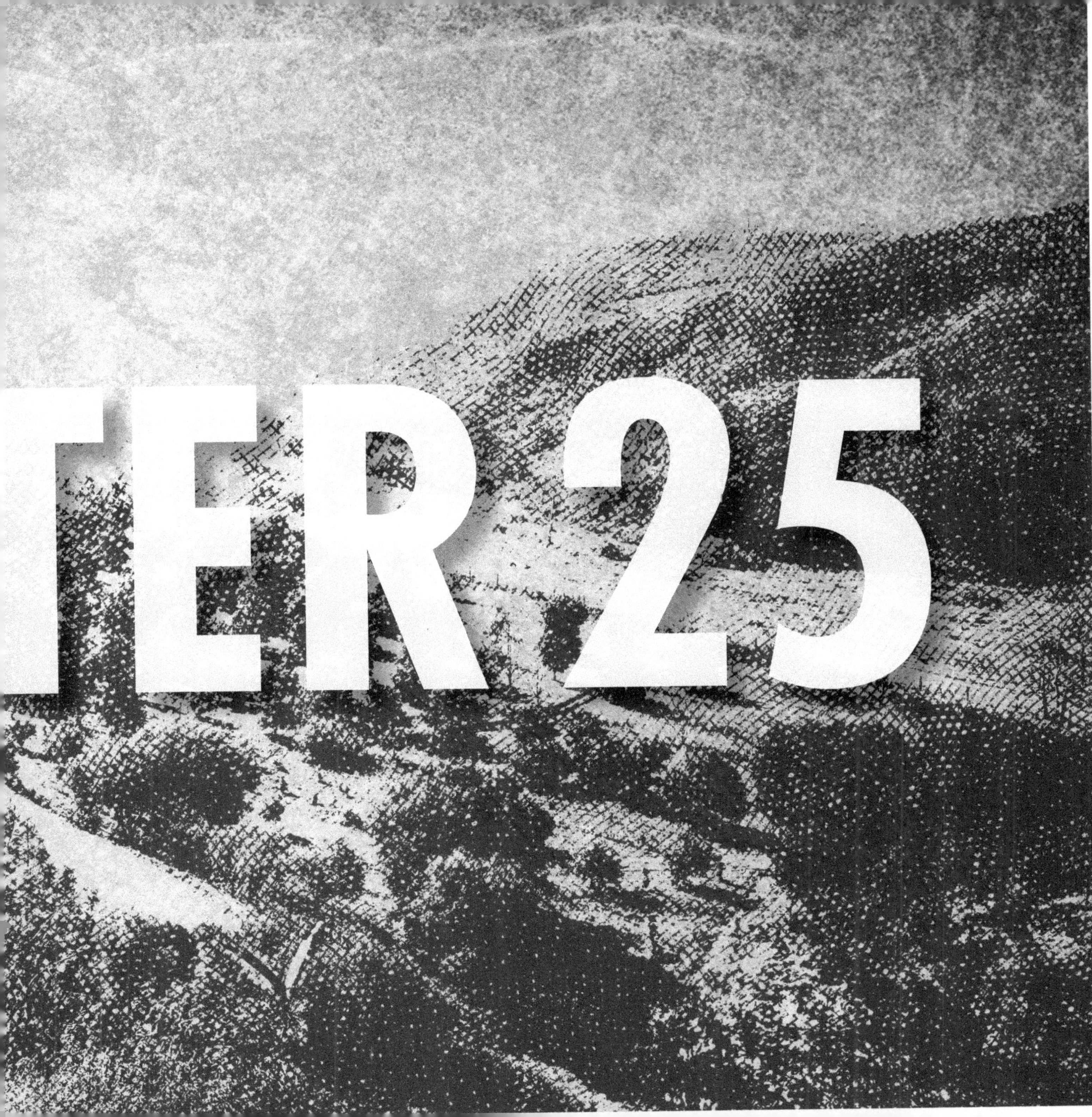

MAYA
BREUER

JANA LONG

YOGA TEACHERS ASSOCIATION

▌ FIRST INTERNATIONAL ASSOCIATION OF BLACK YOGA TEACHERS

In 1999, Krishna Kaur, a successful Black actress during the 1960s and 1970s, and who was introduced to yoga in the mid-70s and became a practitioner of Kundalini yoga under the tutelage of Yogi Bhajan, co-founded the International Association of Black Yoga Teachers and served as its president from 1999 through 2009. (B. 1939).

▌ FIRST BLACK YOGA TEACHERS ASSOCIATION

Founded in 2009, by yoga teachers Maya Breuer and Jana Long, the Black Yoga Teachers Alliance (BYTA) is a social media group that provides a space for yoga practitioners in the U.S. to share information and build a network. Krishna Kaur (International Association of Black Yoga Teachers founder) serves on the BYTA Advisory Council. (B. Unknown).

BUDDHA STATUE

CHAP

CALIFORNIA BOTANICAL GARDENS, 1927

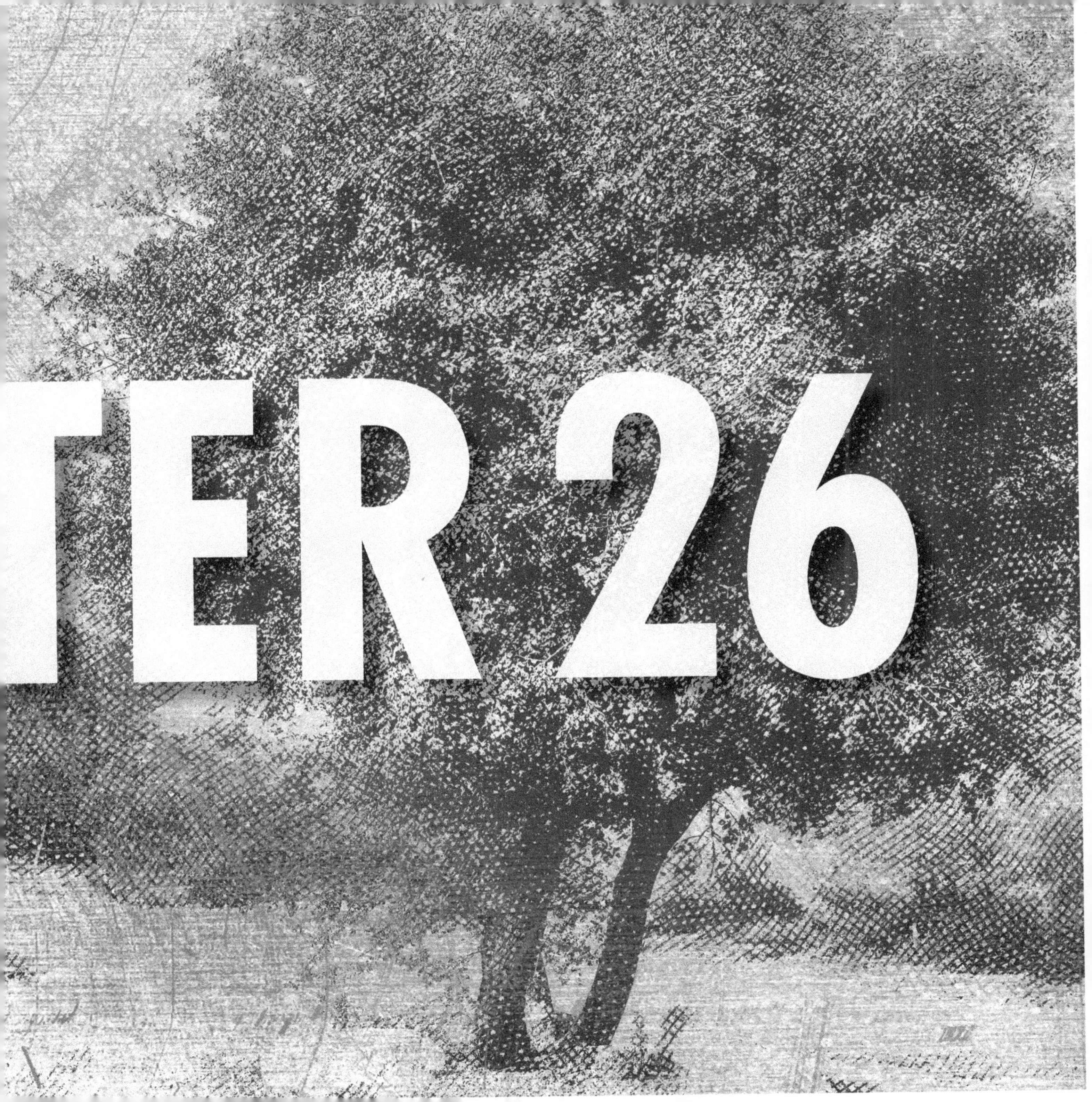
TER 26

DENISE M. VERRET

ZOO DIRECTOR

■ FIRST BLACK DIRECTOR OF LOS ANGELES ZOO AND BOTANICAL GARDENS

In July of 2019 the Los Angeles (LA) City Council confirmed Denise M. Verret to serve as the director of the LA Zoo making Verret both the first Black director of the LA Zoo and Botanical Gardens and the first Black woman to direct an American Zoological Association accredited zoo.

Opened on November 28, 1966, the zoo houses over 1,100 mammals, birds, amphibians and reptiles representing 250 different species; and, the botanical gardens nurture more than 7,400 individual plants representing 800 different species; and both are visited by nearly 1.8 million people annually.

LOS ANGELES ZOO
ENTRY SIGN

VIEW OF HOLLYWOOD, FROM KROTONA HILL, 1900

END NOTES

Black Firsts in Los Angeles was originally part of a larger writing project that examined four questions about Black Los Angeles: (1) Who should people know about; (2) What did they do; (3) When did they do it; (4) Where can people go to learn more about Black people in Los Angeles. The original project became so large that it was necessary to break it up into smaller, more manageable parts resulting in five books: Born in South LA: 100+ Remarkable African Americans Who Were Born, Raised, Lived or Died in South Los Angeles; Go Crenshaw: An Afrocentric Guide to the Crenshaw District; Go South LA: Afrocentric City Guide to South Los Angeles; *Black Firsts in Los Angeles*, California: 190+ Extraordinary Achievements by Afro-Angelenos Listed from A to Z; and, Happened in South LA: An Afrocentric Timeline of Historic Events Impacting Black Life in South Los Angeles, California from 1500 to 2022. If you would like to gain a deeper understanding of Black Los Angeles, please consider perusing all five books.

REFERENCES

ACTORS

Lincoln Perry, Stepin Fetchit, Hollywood's First Black Film Star by Roy Hurst, *National Public Radio* (NPR), *Race, News & Notes*, March 6, 2006, 5:09 PM ET. Accessed 2/15/2023.

Lincoln Perry, the First Black Movie Star by Suzanne Raga. *Retrobituaries, Mental Floss.* February 27, 2019. Accessed 2/15/2023.

Lincoln Perry, Stepin Fetchit, *Wikipedia.* Accessed 2/15/2023.

Sidney Poitier, Who Paved the Way for Black Actors in Film, Dies at 94 by William Grimes, *The New York Times*, January 7, 2022. Accessed 2/15/2023.

Otis Young, 69; First Black to Co-Star in a TV Western Series by Dennis McClellan, Times Staff Writer, *Los Angeles Times*, Television, October 20, 2001, 12AM PT. Accessed 2/16/2023.

ACTORS THEATER

Ebony Theater Tries to Keep Final Curtain From Coming Down by Edward J. Boyer, *Los Angeles Times*, February 1, 1993 12 AM PT.

ACTRESSES

"The First Black Movie Star," Nina Mae McKinney, Gets a Film Retrospective in New York by Craigh Barboza, *The Hollywood Reporter*, November 10, 2021, 8:00 AM. Accessed 2/16/2023.

Nina Mae McKinney, *Wikipedia.* Accessed 2/16/2023.

Dorothy Dandridge, The Dandridge Drama by Mimi Avins, *Los Angeles Times*, August 21, 1999 12 AM PT.

Dorothy Dandridge, *Wikipedia.* Accessed 1/3/2023.

Teresa Graves, Home Fire Kills 'Laugh-In' Star by Eric Malnic, Times Staff Writer, *Los Angeles Times*, October 11, 2002 12 AM PT.

ARCHITECT

Paul R. Williams, Black History is L.A. History: A guide to public places and spaces showcasing the impact of African Americans on Los Angeles, African American Heritage Map by L.A. Controller Ron Galperin.

Paul R. Williams, FAIA, (1894-1980), Los Angeles Conservancy. Accessed 11/22/2022.

Paul R. Williams, Angelus Funeral Home History by John Hill III, President of Angelus Funeral Home. angelusfuneralhome.com. Accessed 11/18/2022.

Paul R. Williams, List of Los Angeles Historic-Cultural Monuments, *Wikipedia.* Accessed 11/16/22.

An encore for the historic Dunbar Hotel by Bob Pool, *Los Angeles Times*, June 11, 2013 12 AM PT.

ARTISTS

Beulah Ecton Woodard, Visual Arts, African American History of Los Angeles, Los Angeles Citywide Historic Context Statement, *Los Angeles Historic Resources Survey*, Prepared for: City of Los Angeles, Department of City Planning, Office of Historic Resources. Page 204.

Beulah Ecton Woodard, Review: For the Black artists of CAAM's 'L.A. Blacksmith,' metal has meaning by Christopher Knight, Art Critic, *Los Angeles Times*, September 27, 2019 7 AM PT.

Beulah Ecton Woodard, *Wikipedia.* Accessed 1/5/2023.

Alice Patrick, 14 Black Muralists in LA You Need To Know, Social and Public Art Resource Center, July 25, 2020. Accessed 1/9/2023.

Alice Patrick, *Wikipedia.* Accessed 12/22/2022.

ART EXHIBITIONS

First Black Art Exhibit, Visual Arts, African American History of Los Angeles, Los Angeles Citywide Historic Context Statement, *Los Angeles Historic Resources Survey*, Prepared for: City of Los Angeles, Department of City Planning, Office of Historic Resources. Page 203.

The First Black American Art Exhibit in Los Angeles, 1929 by Eric J. Merrell. Ericmerrell.com. Accessed 12/22/2022.

Review: For the Black artists of CAAM's 'L.A. Blacksmith,' metal has meaning by Christopher Knight, Art Critic, *Los Angeles Times*, September 27, 2019 7 AM PT.

Gallery 32 and Los Angeles's African American Arts Community by Carolyn Peter and Damon Willick, *Journal of Contemporary African Art*, 30, Spring 2012, DOI 10.1215/10757163-1496435, Nka Publications.

First Group Exhibition of Black Women Artists, Visual Arts, African American History of Los Angeles, Los Angeles Citywide Historic Context Statement, *Los Angeles Historic Resources Survey*, Prepared for: City of Los Angeles, Department of City Planning, Office of Historic Resources. Page 209.

Two Centuries of Black American Art, Los Angeles County Museum of Art, September 30 to November 21, 1976. Organized by the

Los Angeles County Museum of Art. Guest curator: David C. Driskell.

AVIATORS

Black Wings: The Life of African American Aviation Pioneer William Powell, National Air and Space Museum, Smithsonian, Institute, February 2, 2016. Accessed 6/13/2023.

Early Black Pilot Found Racial Equality in the Sky by Cecelia Rasmussen, *Los Angeles Times*, November 5, 2000 12 AM PT.

William J. Powell - Black Aviation Pioneer, *Los Angeles Almanac*. Accessed 1/6/2023.

Blackbirds and the Colored Air Circus of 1931 by Phil Scott. Air Facts, the journal for personal air travel by pilots for pilots. June 1, 2012. Accessed 2/9/2023.

James Banning and Thomas Allen, 10 African American Pioneers of Aviation and Aerospace by Airport Staff, Dayton International Airport, General News, February 8, 2021. Accessed 2/15/2023.

James Banning and Thomas Allen, Banning, James Herman (1900–1933) by Oklahoma Historical Society, The Encyclopedia of Oklahoma History and Culture. Accessed 2/15/2023.

BANKER

Onie B. Granville, Remembering Onie B. Granville, Founder of First Black Owned Commercial Bank in California by LA Urban League, May 14, 2022, President Message, Los Angeles Urban League. Accessed 11/18/2022.

The (Los Angeles) Bank of Finance (1964-1981) by Nancy Mallard. *Black Past*. August 15, 2018. Accessed 2/9/2023.

BARBERSHOP OWNER

Peter Biggs, African American History of Los Angeles, Los Angeles Citywide Historic Context Statement, *Los Angeles Historic Resources Survey*, Prepared for: City of Los Angeles, Department of City Planning,

Office of Historic Resources, February 2018. Accessed 12/7/2022. Page 10.

Peter Biggs, This Immigrant Came to California Enslaved and Died a Thriving Entrepreneur by John Greathouse, *Forbes*, July 26, 2019. Accessed 12/29/2022.

On this Day: The Assassination of Abraham Lincoln and Reaction in Los Angeles, 14 April 1865 by Paul R. Spitzzeri, *Homestead Museum* Posted on April 14, 2017. Accessed 6.13.2023.

BASKETBALL COACHES

(Larry Farmer) The Greatest Bruin You Don't Know by Delan Bruce, *UCLA Magazine*, Newsroom, March 21, 2023. Accessed 6.16.2023.

Larry Farmer (basketball), *Wikipedia*. Accessed 2/27/2023.

Former USC Coach George Raveling elected into Basketball Hall of Fame by Mike Bresnahan, *Los Angeles Times*, February 14, 2015, 9:30 AM PT.

Cheryl Miller Receives an Offer to Coach USC by Elliott Almond, USC Sports, *Los Angeles Times*, September 2, 1993, 12 AM PT. Accessed 2/28/2023.

Lakers add former WNBA player Shay Murphy as coaching associate by Kurt Helin, NBA, NBC Sports, October 3, 2021, 9:19 AM EDT. Accessed 2/28/2023.

WNBA champion Shay Murphy comes back to Los Angeles as first woman coach for the Lakers by Colby Martin, Jameela Hammond, Yuki Liang and Aarohi Sheth, *USC Annenberg Media*, April 28, 2022 at 7:16 pm PDT. Accessed 2/28/2023.

BASKETBALL STAR

Black History Month: Don Barksdale achieved many firsts on and off the basketball court by Jason Lewis, Sports Editor, *Los Angeles Sentinel*, Published February 27, 2013.

Don Barksdale, *Wikipedia*. Accessed February 7, 2023.

BEAUTY SCHOOL FOUNDER

Hazel Dell Williams; Founder of Early Beauty School for Blacks, L.A. Times Archives, *Los Angeles Times*, February 20, 1988, 12 AM PT

BLOOD BANK

Inter-Racial Blood Bank at Rose-Netta Hospital, African American History of Los Angeles, Los Angeles Citywide Historic Context Statement, *Los Angeles Historic Resources Survey*, Prepared for: City of Los Angeles, Department of City Planning, Office of Historic Resources, February 2018. Accessed 12/7/2022. Page 155.

Charles R. Drew, Becoming "the Father of the Blood Bank," 1938-1941, The Charles R. Drew Papers, National Institute of Health, National Library of Medicine, *Profiles in Science*. Accessed 3/6/2023.

BOARD OF SUPERVISORS MEMBERS

Yvonne Brathwaite Burke, Awaiting a Winner: Board of Supervisors: Yvonne Brathwaite Burke leads Diane Watson by 775 votes with uncounted absentee ballots to determine the outcome. By Frederick M. Muir and Richard Simon, Times Staff Writers, *Los Angeles Times*, November 5, 1992.

Mark Ridley-Thomas, Los Angeles County Supervisor Mark Ridley-Thomas declares victory in 10th District by David Zahniser, *Los Angeles Times*, November 3, 2020.

Mark Ridley-Thomas, LA Councilman Mark Ridley-Thomas and his wife, Avis, honored for 30 years of service, Avis & Mark Ridley-Thomas Wellness Center christened at Charles R. Drew University by David Crane, *Los Angeles Daily News*, September 16, 2021.

BUS DRIVER

Mrs. Arcola Philpott, Celebrating Black History Month: How The First African-

American Motormen & "Motormanette" Pioneered Social Justice On The Los Angeles Railway by Metro Digital Resources Librarian, February 9, 2011. Accessed 2/7/2023.

BUSINESS OWNERS

The Owens Block (Robert Curry Owens), The New American Outpost, *Los Angeles Almanac*, History Timeline, Los Angeles County, 1848 to 1865. Accessed 11/16/2022.

Biddy Mason, *Wikipedia*. Accessed 12/23/2022.

Angelus Funeral Home History by John Hill III, President of Angelus Funeral Home. angelus-funeralhome.com. Accessed 11/18/2022.

Angelus Funeral Home, List of Los Angeles Historic-Cultural Monuments, *Wikipedia*. Accessed 11/16/22.

Angelus Funeral Home History by John Hill III, President of Angelus Funeral Home. angelus-funeralhome.com. Accessed 11/18/2022.

Porter-Roberts Company (Funeral Home), African American History of Los Angeles, Los Angeles Citywide Historic Context Statement, *Los Angeles Historic Resources Survey*, Prepared for: City of Los Angeles, Department of City Planning, Office of Historic Resources, February 2018. Accessed 12/7/2022. Pages 62.

CALIFORNIA STATE POLITICAL REPRESENTATIVES FROM LOS ANGELES

Hon. Frederick Madison Roberts – California's First African American Legislator, 1919-1934, California State Assembly, California Legislative Black Caucus website. Accessed 11/16/2022.

Frederick Madison Roberts, *Wikipedia*. Accessed 11/30/2022.

Dymally, Mervyn Malcolm, History, Art & Archives, United States House of Representatives, history.house.gov. Accessed 12/21/2022.

Karen Bass, First black woman to lead state Assembly by Nancy Vogel, Times Staff Writer, *Los Angeles Times*, February. 29, 2008 8 AM PT.

Mervyn Dymally, A pioneer for black lawmakers in L.A. by Claudia Luther and Valerie J. Nelson, Special to the Times, *Los Angeles Times*, November 13, 2007 12 AM PT.

CHEMISTS

Grant D. Venerable, African American Heritage in Science, Engineering and Medicine in Los Angeles, *Los Angeles Almanac*. Accessed 11/16/2022.

James E. LuValle, African American Heritage in Science, Engineering and Medicine in Los Angeles, *Los Angeles Almanac*. Accessed 11/16/2022.

James E. LuValle (1912-1993), *Black Past*. Contributed by Robert Fikes, January 23, 2007. Accessed 1/12/2023.

CHILD ACTORS

Ernest Frederick Morrison, 'Little Rascal' Player Ernest Morrison Dies by Davan Maharaj, Times Staff Writer, *Los Angeles Times*, July 31, 1989, 12 AM PT.

Ernest Frederick Morrison (1912-1989) by Euell A. Nielson, *Black Past*, June 27, 2020. Accessed 3/28/2023.

Ernest Frederick Morrison, Meet The First Black Child Star Of The 1920s by ZamaMdoda, *AfroPunk*, May 31, 2019. Accessed 3/28/2023.

Matthew 'Stymie' Beard Jr, *Wikipedia*. Accessed 3.28.2023.

Allen 'Farina' Hoskins, *Wikipedia*. Accessed 3.28.2023.

William Billie 'Buckwheat' Thomas Jr., Contributed by Samuel Momodu, *Black Past*, January 21, 2023. Accessed 3.28.2023.

CHURCHES

First African Methodist Episcopal Church, National Museum of African American History and Culture, Westward Expansion and Freedom of Expression, SearchableMuseum. com. Accessed 3/28/2023.

First African Methodist Episcopal Church, African American History of Los Angeles, Los Angeles Citywide Historic Context Statement, Page 105, *Los Angeles Historic Resources Survey*, Prepared for: City of Los Angeles, Department of City Planning, Office of Historic Resources, February 2018. Accessed 12/7/2022.

First African Methodist Episcopal Church, *Wikipedia*. Accessed 3.28.2023.

Archbishop Carl Bean, 'beacon of light' in LGBTQ church movement and AIDS activism, dies by Marissa Evans and Gregory Yee, Times Staff Writers, *Los Angeles Times*, September. 9, 2021 1:57 PM PT.

Carl Bean, Good News at Unity : For Carl Bean, Rejection by His Childhood Church Pointed the Way to a New Ministry by Carol Chastang, Times Staff Writer, *Los Angeles Times*, October. 5, 1992 12 AM PT.

Carl Bean, *Wikipedia*. Accessed 12/7/2022.

CITY COUNCIL MEMBERS

Gilbert Lindsay, From the Archives: Gilbert Lindsay, 1st L.A. Black Councilman, Dies by Janet Clayton and Tracy Wilkinson, Times Staff Writers, *Los Angeles Times*, December 29, 1990 12 AM PT.

Gilbert William Lindsay (1900-1990), Contributed by Martin Schiesl, *Black Past*. Accessed 12/8/2022.

Gilbert W. Lindsay, *Wikipedia*. Accessed 12/8/2022.

Gilbert W. Lindsay, Billy Mills and Tom Bradley, History Timeline, Los Angeles County, 1963 to 1979, America's New Big City, *Los Angeles Almanac*. Accessed 11/18/2022.

Douglas Dollarhide, Former mail carrier became first black mayor of Compton by Esmeralda Bermudez, Times Staff Writer, *Los Angeles Times*, July 9, 2008.

Mark Ridley-Thomas and Rita Walters, Mantle Passes to City's New Black Leaders: Election: Ridley-Thomas and Walters vow to break with policies of predecessors on City Council and focus on residents' needs. By John L. Mitchell and Laurie Becklund, Times Staff Writers, *Los Angeles Times*, June 6, 1991.

Rita Walters, a fierce advocate for equality and trailblazing elected official, dies at 89 by Howard Blume, Staff Writer, *Los Angeles Times*, February. 20, 2020 10:44 PM PT.

CONGRESSIONAL REPRESENTATIVES

Augustus Hawkins, A pioneer for black lawmakers in L.A. by Claudia Luther and Valerie J. Nelson, Special to the Times, *Los Angeles Times*, November 13, 2007 12 AM PT.

Augustus Hawkins, *Wikipedia*. Accessed 11/30/2022.

Yvonne Brathwaite Burke, History, Art & Archives, U.S. House of Representatives, history.house.gov. Accessed 12/8/2022.

Yvonne Brathwaite Burke, *Wikipedia*. Accessed 12/8/2022.

COOKIE KING

Wally Amos, 'Famous Amos' meets local fans by Kelly Strodl, Southern California, Daily Pilot, *Los Angeles Times*, August. 28, 2006 12 AM PT.

Wally Amos, How Wally Amos Made Famous Amos Cookies So Famous — With A Little Help From Marvin Gaye by Hadley Meares, LA History, *LAist*, Published August 13, 2019, 6:00 AM. Accessed 12/16/22.

CORONER

Dr. Odey C. Ukpo, LA County appoints Ukpo as interim coroner by *City News Service*, *Los Angeles Daily News*. Published: November 6, 2022 at 10:46 a.m. Updated: November 6 2022 at 10:50 a.m.

DENTAL SCHOOL GRADUATE/S

John Alexander Somerville and Vada Watson Somerville, Trojan Tales: USC's First Black Graduate and the Representation of Diversity in the School of Dentistry by Josh Paybera, *USC Annenberg Media*, October 05, 2016 at 4:52 am PDT.

John Alexander Somerville and Vada Watson Somerville, A Pioneer of Black Los Angeles, by Cecilia Rasmussen, Times Staff Writer, *Los Angeles Times*, December 23, 1996.

Vada Watson Somerville, *Wikipedia*. Accessed 2/28/2023.

Dr. Linda Lott, UCLA Student National Dental Association. Facebook. Accessed 8/8/2023.

DENTISTS

Alva Curtis Garrott, D.D.S., African American History of Los Angeles, Los Angeles Citywide Historic Context Statement, *Los Angeles Historic Resources Survey*, Prepared for: City of Los Angeles, Department of City Planning, Office of Historic Resources, February 2018. Accessed 12/7/2022. Page 151.

A Family's Fight: The Challenge of Being Black in Glendale; Dr. Alva Garrott and Lillie De Jarnette Garrott. *ReflectSpace.org*. Accessed 8/7/2023.

John Alexander Somerville and Vada Watson Somerville, A Pioneer of Black Los Angeles, by Cecilia Rasmussen, Times Staff Writer, *Los Angeles Times*, December 23, 1996.

Vada Watson Somerville (1885-1972): African-American Pioneer. Sindecuse Museum, School of Dentistry, University of Michigan. Accessed 8/7/2023.

DISTRICT ATTORNEYS

Leon Whitaker, List of First Minority Male Lawyers and Judges in California, *Wikipedia*. Accessed 12/20/2022.

Whitaker, Leon L., 1904-1931, Six charter members of the Kappa Alpha Psi fraternity in

the UCLA Yearbook, 1924, Miriam Matthews Photograph Collection, UCLA Library Digital Collections. Accessed 12/20/2022.

Marion L. Obera, List of First Women Lawyers and Judges in California, *Wikipedia*. Accessed 12/20/2022.

Marion L. Obera, On-Time Justice Is Judge's Policy : 'Maximum Marion' Given Credit for Most Productive Courtroom by Terry Pristin, Times Staff Writer, *Los Angeles Times*, December 28, 1986, 12 AM PT.

Johnnie Cochran, Flashy, Deft Lawyer Known Worldwide by Carla Hall, *Los Angeles Times*, March 30, 2005 12 AM PT.

Consuelo Bland Marshall, *Wikipedia*. Accessed 1/3/2023.

Consuelo Bland Marshall, List of First Women Lawyers and Judges in California, *Wikipedia*. Accessed 12/20/2022.

Jackie Lacey, Black Lives matter's surprising target: Los Angeles county's first black district attorney by Stephanie Elam and Jason Kravarik, CNN.com. Updated 9:18 PM EDT, Wednesday July 15, 2020. Accessed 12/20/2022.

Jackie Lacey takes office as county's first female, black D.A. by Jack Leonard, Senior Editor, Investigations, *Los Angeles Times*, December. 3, 2012

DOCTORS

Dr. Monroe Alpheus Majors, African American Heritage in Science, Engineering and Medicine in Los Angeles, *Los Angeles Almanac*. Accessed 11/16/2022.

Ruth Janetta Temple, African American History of Los Angeles, Los Angeles Citywide Historic Context Statement, *Los Angeles Historic Resources Survey*, Prepared for: City of Los Angeles, Department of City Planning, Office of Historic Resources, February 2018. Accessed 12/7/2022. Page 154.

Ruth Janetta Temple, African American Heritage in Science, Engineering and Medicine in Los Angeles, *Los Angeles Almanac*. Accessed 11/16/2022.

Leonard Stovall, African American History of Los Angeles, Los Angeles Citywide Historic Context Statement, *Los Angeles Historic Resources Survey*, Prepared for: City of Los Angeles, Department of City Planning, Office of Historic Resources, February 2018. Accessed 12/7/2022. Page 154.

Raleigh Bledsoe, Kaiser Permanente, Who we are, Our history, Raleigh Bledsoe MD: First Black physician for Southern California Permanente Group. First Black radiologist west of Rockies. January 21, 2014. Accessed 2/14/2023.

ENVIRONMENTAL HEALTH ADMINISTRATOR

Erica Blyther, New administrator balances needs of residents, oil industry by Sue Favor, contributing Writer, *Los Angeles Wave Newspapers*, June 18, 2021. Accessed 2/10/2023.

EXECUTIVE OFFICER

Fesia Davenport Appointed First Black Chief Executive Officer to Serve LA County by *Black Voice News*, January 14, 2021. Accessed 2/10/2023.

FILM DIRECTOR

John Singleton, How 'Boyz N the Hood' Shined a Spotlight on This South L.A. Street 30 Years Ago: Three decades ago, John Singleton's groundbreaking film turned Cimarron Street into a beloved L.A. landmark—and it's still celebrated today. By Jared Cowan, *Los Angeles Magazine*, July 7, 2021.

John Singleton, Boyz N the Hood, Academy Museum of Motion Pictures, August 23, 2022. Accessed 11/16/2022.

John Singleton, How John Singleton Made History as the Oscars' First Black Best Director Nominee: With "Boyz n the Hood,"

he broke down barriers for black filmmakers with Oscar nominations, commercial success, and the creation of an entirely new genre. By Tambay Obenson, IndieWire, April 29, 2019.

John Singleton, Filmmaker John Singleton dies; 'Boyz n the Hood' was his own personal L.A. story by Sonaiya Kelley, *Los Angeles Times*, April 29, 2019.

John Singleton: A Celebration, September 9, 2022 - April 19, 2023, 7:00 P.M., Cinema.USC.Edu. Accessed 8/25/2023.

FIREFIGHTERS

Sam Haskins, Project Roll Call, National Fallen Firefighters Foundation. Accessed 1/6/2023.

Sam Haskins, Stentorians, *Wikipedia*. Accessed 1/6/2023.

Sam Haskins, *The Los Angeles Fire Department Historical Archive*, History of the Black Firemen, The Segregated Years, October 1897 to September 1956. Accessed 1/6/2023.

George Bright, *The Los Angeles Fire Department Historical Archive*, History of the Black Firemen, The Segregated Years, October 1897 to September 1956. Accessed 1/6/2023.

George Bright, Stentorians, *Wikipedia*. Accessed 1/6/2023.

Robert Lee, County's First Black Battalion Chief, Passes Away by Sentinel News Service, *Los Angeles Sentinel*, Published July 7, 2022.

Kristine Larsen, First female LAFD African American captain promoted to battalion chief by *Daily News*. Published: February 16, 2017 at 9:49 p.m. Updated: August 28, 2017 at 5:45 a.m. Accessed 2/10/2023.

Daryl Osby, L.A. County Fire Dept. swears in first black chief by *Daily Breeze*. Published: February 17, 2011 at 12:00 a.m. Updated: September 6, 2017 at 8:40 a.m. Accessed 2/10/2023.

FOOTBALL COACHES

Brice Union Taylor (1902-1974) contributed by Jeremy Sadwoski, *Black Past*, November 2, 2015. Accessed 2/27/2023.

Art Shell, The Raiders Are Back--Thanks to Shell : Football: Lester Hayes thought Shell could do it. And now the team is believing it too. By Michael Wilbon, The *Washington Post*, *Los Angeles Times*, November 15, 1989 12 AM PT.

Art Shell Reflects on Becoming NFL's 1st Black Head Coach in the Modern Era by Mike Freeman, *Bleacher Report*, October 9, 2014. Accessed 1/3/2023.

Art Shell, *Wikipedia*. Accessed 3/7/2023.

UCLA Hires Karl Dorrell As Football Coach by John Nadel, *Midland Daily News*, December 18, 2002. Accessed 2/28/2023.

(Donte Williams) USC Interim head coach Donte Williams, makes history as Trojans first Black head football coach. *City News Service*, *Los Angeles Sentinel*, September 16, 2021. Accessed 2/28/2023.

FOOTBALL STARS

Brice Union Taylor, USC BLack Alumni Association Timeline, University of Southern California Black Alumni Association. alumni.usc.edu/baa/timeline. Accessed 12/20/2022.

Brice Union Taylor, *Wikipedia*. Accessed 1/9/2023.

The Black Bruins: The Remarkable Lives of UCLA's Jackie Robinson, Woody Strode, Tom Bradley, Kenny Washington and Ray Barlett by James W. Johnson, *University of Nebraska Press*. Copyright 2017.

Kenny Washington, *Britannica.com*. Accessed 1/5/2023.

Kenny Washington, *Wikipedia*. Accessed 1/5/2023.

Woody Strode, *Wikipedia*. Accessed 1/5/2023.

Mike Garrett, *Wikipedia*. Accessed 12/20/2022.

GOVERNOR AND LIEUTENANT GOVERNOR

Pío Pico, Afro Latinos and the development of early California, U.S. *National Park Service*, Department of the Interior, African Americans in Los Angeles, People. Accessed 11/9/2022.

Pio Pico, History of African Americans in Los Angeles, *Wikipedia*. Accessed 12/21/2022.

Dymally, Mervyn Malcolm, History, Art & Archives, United States House of Representatives, history.house.gov. Accessed 12/21/2022.

GRAND JURY CHAIRPERSON

Jesse (Lee) Robinson; Pioneering Black Civic Leader by Myrna Oliver, Times Staff Writer, *Los Angeles Times*, June 16, 1993 12 AM PT.

Jesse Lee Robinson, A Hero in His Own Town : Jesse Robinson, Compton's Favorite Resident, Honored by Park in His Name by Terry Spencer, Times Staff Writer, *Los Angeles Times*, December 6, 1987 12 AM PT.

HAMBURGER QUEEN

Lovie Yancey, Fatburger founder expanded South L.A. eatery into chain by Dennis Mclellan, Times Staff Writer, *Los Angeles Times*, February 2, 2008 12 AM PT.

From South L.A. hamburger joint to franchise, First black mayor, Fatburger founder: These are some snapshots from L.A.'s black history by *Los Angeles Times* Staff, *Los Angeles Times*, February. 23, 2016 9:43 P.M.

HEAD OF HOUSEHOLD

Peter Biggs, African American History of Los Angeles, Los Angeles Citywide Historic Context Statement, *Los Angeles Historic Resources Survey*, Prepared for: City of Los Angeles, Department of City Planning, Office of Historic Resources, February 2018. Page

10. Accessed 12/7/2022.

HELICOPTER PILOT

Anthony Pachot dies; L.A. County sheriff's first black copter pilot by Bob Pool, *Los Angeles Times*, February 18, 2013 12 AM PT.

Long Beach Police Department pilot alleges racial discrimination on the job by Kate Cagle, *Long Beach, Spectrum News 1*, Published 5:00 PM PT, February 17, 2022. Accessed 2/13/2023.

HIGHWAY PATROLMAN

Homer Garrott; Judge, 1st Black CHP Officer, L.A. Times Archives, *Los Angeles Times*, March 20, 1998, 12 AM PT.

Homer L. Garrott (1915-1998), Contributed by Dai'Quiriya Martinez, *Black Past*, November 22, 2017. Accessed 2/17/2023.

HIV POSITIVE PROFESSIONAL ATHLETE

Magic Johnson to Rejoin Lakers Despite HIV by Mark Heisler, Times Staff Writer, *Los Angeles Times*, September 30, 1992 12 AM PT.

HOLLYWOOD CORRESPONDENT

Fay M. Jackson, Fay M. Jackson and the Color Line: The First African American Foreign Correspondent for the Associated Negro Press by Lae'l Hughes-Watkins. Published 2009, History, *The Journal of Pan-African Studies*.

Fay M. Jackson, USC BLack Alumni Association Timeline, University of Southern California Black Alumni Association. alumni.usc.edu/baa/timeline. Accessed 12/20/2022.

Fay M. Jackson, *Wikipedia*. Accessed 12/20/2022.

HOSPITALS

Dunbar Hospital, African American History of Los Angeles, Los Angeles Citywide Historic Context Statement, *Los Angeles Historic Resources Survey*, Prepared for: City of Los Angeles, Department of City Planning,

Office of Historic Resources, February 2018. Accessed 12/7/2022. Page 153.

West View Hospital, Los Angeles, CA, Gallery, PaulRWilliamsProject.Org. Accessed 9/8/2023.

Rose-Netta Hospital, African American History of Los Angeles, Los Angeles Citywide Historic Context Statement, *Los Angeles Historic Resources Survey*, Prepared for: City of Los Angeles, Department of City Planning, Office of Historic Resources, February 2018. Accessed 12/7/2022. Page 155.

King, Norris Curtis, From NKAA, Notable Kentucky African Americans Database (main entry). Accessed 3/8/2023.

HOUSING SPECIALIST

Jessie L. Terry, African American History of Los Angeles, Los Angeles Citywide Historic Context Statement, *Los Angeles Historic Resources Survey*, Prepared for: City of Los Angeles, Department of City Planning, Office of Historic Resources, February 2018. Accessed 12/7/2022. Pages 227.

INVENTOR

Dr. Patricia Bath, African American Heritage in Science, Engineering and Medicine in Los Angeles, *Los Angeles Almanac*. Accessed 11/16/2022.

Dr. Patricia Bath, *Wikipedia*. Accessed 1/5/2023.

Patricia Bath, *Biography.com*. January, 7, 2021. Accessed 8/8/2023.

JANITORS

Lewis G. Green: A Pioneer of the Black Community of Los Angeles, 1850s-1880s by Paul R. Spitzzeri, *Homestead Museum*, The Homestead Blog, Posted on February 23, 2017.

Gilbert Lindsay, From the Archives: Gilbert Lindsay, 1st L.A. Black Councilman, Dies by Janet Clayton and Tracy Wilkinson, Times

Staff Writers, *Los Angeles Times*, December 29, 1990 12 AM PT.

JOB KING

John Wesley Coleman, The Transcontinental Railroad, African Americans and the California Dream by Alison Rose Jefferson, June 17, 2019. *California Historical Society*. Accessed February 8, 2023.

JUDGES

Thomas Griffith Jr., Pioneering Black Lawyer, Judge Dies, L.A. Times Archives, *Los Angeles Times*, March 7, 1986 12 AM PT.

Vaino Spencer, Historic Women Behind the Bench and Badge Los Angeles County, Crime & Justice, *Los Angeles Almanac*. Accessed 1/13/2023.

Vaino Spencer, List of First Women Lawyers and Judges in California, *Wikipedia*. Accessed 12/20/2022.

Maxine F. Thomas, List of First Women Lawyers and Judges in California, *Wikipedia*. Accessed 12/20/2022.

Arleigh M. Woods, African American Women Appeal Court Justices by Yussuf Simmonds (Managing Editor), *Los Angeles Sentinel*, Published March 29, 2012.

Arleigh M. Woods, Historic Women Behind the Bench and Badge Los Angeles County, Crime & Justice, *Los Angeles Almanac*. Accessed 1/13/2023.

Arleigh M. Woods, List of First Women Lawyers and Judges in California, *Wikipedia*. Accessed 12/20/2022.

Judge Kevin Brazile, First African American Presiding Judge of Los Angeles Superior Court, Honored by UCLA Black Alumni Association, National Association for Presiding Judges and Court Executive Officers, Source: UBAA, March 1, 2019, NAPCO4Courtleaders.org. Accessed 12/20/2022.

Los Angeles - Judges Elect Kevin C. Brazile Presiding Judge and Eric C. Taylor Asst. Presiding Judge, legalprofessionalsinc.org. Accessed 12/20/2022.

JUDICIAL OVERSEER

Ann Shaw, Trailblazing LA Civic Leader, Passes Away by Cora Jackson-Fossett Sentinel Religion Editor, *Los Angeles Sentinel*, Published May 14, 2015.

Ann Shaw dies at 93; civic leader in Los Angeles for five decades by Elaine Woo, Writer, *Los Angeles Times*, May 11, 2015 8:45 PM PT.

Ann Shaw (social worker), *Wikipedia*. Accessed 1/3/2023.

Commission on Judicial Performance, State of California. CJP.CA.GOV. Accessed 8/8/2023.

KARATE SCHOOLS

Black Dragon: Afro Asian Performance and the Martial Arts Imagination by Zachary F. Price, Black Performance and Cultural Criticism, E. Patrick Johnson, Series Editor, *Published by The Ohio State University Press*, Copyright 2022 by Zachary F. Price.

Our Fist is Black: Martial Arts, Black Arts, and Black power in the 1960s and 1970s by Maryam Aziz. *ChineseMartialArtsStudies.com*. Accessed 2/22/23.

Black Karate Federation, *bkfwarriors.org*, stories, black-karate-federation, 10/2/2020. Accessed 2/22/23.

LABOR LEADERS

Buddy Collette, *Wikiepedia*. Accessed 8/8/2023.

Black History Month Labor Profiles: Arlene Holt Baker by Kenneth Quinnell, *AFL-CIO. ORG*. February 8, 2019. Accessed 8/8/2023.

Yvonne Wheeler, After racist leak, L.A. County Fed finds a new leader to repair damaged relationships by Suhauna Hussain, Staff Writer, *Los Angeles Times*, November 22, 2022 5:07 PM PT.

LAWYERS

Robert Charles O'Hara Benjamin, List of First Minority Male Lawyers and Judges in California, *Wikipedia*. Accessed 12/20/2022.

Robert Charles O'Hara Benjamin, Black History Month: The life of Robert Charles O'Hara Benjamin by Taylor Pettit, TPETTIT@HERALD-LEADER.COM, *Lexington Herald-Leader*, Updated November 12, 2015 1:15 PM.

Thomas Griffith Jr., Pioneering Black Lawyer, Judge Dies, L.A. Times Archives, *Los Angeles Times*, March 7, 1986 12 AM PT.

Samuel L. Williams, List of First Minority Male Lawyers and Judges in California, *Wikipedia*. Accessed 12/20/2022.

Samuel L. Williams, *Wikipedia*. Accessed 12/20/2022.

LAW SCHOOL GRADUATES

Clarence Bertrand Thompson, USC BLack Alumni Association Timeline, University of Southern California Black Alumni Association. alumni.usc.edu/baa/timeline. Accessed 12/20/2022.

Helen Wheeler Riddle, USC BLack Alumni Association Timeline, University of Southern California Black Alumni Association. alumni.usc.edu/baa/timeline. Accessed 12/20/2022.

Billy G. Mills, *Wikipedia*. Accessed 12/7/2022.

LIBRARIAN

Miriam Matthews, 97; Pioneering L.A. Librarian Was an Expert in Black History by Myrna Oliver,Times Staff Writer, *Los Angeles Times*, July 6, 2003 12 AM PT.

California Library Hall of Fame: Miriam Matthews (1905-2003), *California Library Association*. Accessed 8/25/2023.

LIFEGUARD

First Black Lifeguard Working to Blaze Trail : Diversity: Russell Walker was first hired in 1965 and recently was promoted to captain. He has helped found a program to encourage inner-city youths to pursue ocean-related careers. By Kathleen Kelleher, Special to the Times, *Los Angeles Times*, March 28, 1993, 12 AM PT.

MARATHON ORGANIZER

Bill Burke, Marathon Inc. : Businessman Bill Burke Is No Athlete. But He Knows How to Run a Race. By Greg Critser, *Los Angeles Times*, February 22, 1987 12 AM PT.

Bill Burke, L.A. Race Running on Influence: Marathon: Political friendships have helped Burke turn fledgling venture into marketing success. By Julie Cart, Times Staff Writer, *Los Angeles Times*, March 1, 1991 12 AM PT.

MAYORS

Juan Francisco Reyes, Afro-Mexicans in Early Los Angeles: Exhibit Postscript by UCLA Library, Library Special Collections Blog, 2/26/2015.

Juan Francisco Reyes (CA. 1749-CA. 1800), *Black Past*, contributed by John W. Ravage, February 12, 2008.

Douglas Dollarhide Dies, by Yussuf Simmonds (Managing Editor), *Los Angeles Sentinel*, Published July 10, 2008.

Douglas Dollarhide, Compton's first Black mayor remembered as trailblazer by Betty Pleasant, Contributing Editor, *Los Angeles Wave*, July 10, 2008.

Douglas Dollarhide, Former mail carrier became first black mayor of Compton by Esmeralda Bermudez, Times Staff Writer, *Los Angeles Times*, July 9, 2008.

Doris Davis, Memorial Set for Doris Davis, Compton's First Black Female Mayor by Staff and Wire Report, *Los Angeles Sentinel*, Published March 1, 2018.

Tom Bradley, From the Archives: Mayor Who Reshaped L.A. Dies by Jean Merl and Bill Boyarsky, *Los Angeles Times*, September. 30, 1998 5 AM PT.

Tom Bradley, From the Archives: Open Doors at City Hall by Scott Harrison, *Los Angeles Times*, March 5, 2017 1 AM PT.

Edward Vincent dies at 78; first black mayor of Inglewood by Valerie J. Nelson, *Los Angeles Times*, September 5, 2012.

Rex Richardson, Long Beach to elect first Black mayor, Rex Richardson, after opponent concedes by Alexandra E. Petri, Staff Writer, *Los Angeles Times*, November 15, 2022, 9:45 AM PT.

Karen Bass elected, becoming L.A.'s first woman mayor by Julia Wick, Staff Writer, *Los Angeles Times*, November 16, 2022, 3:52 PM PT.

MEDICAL SCHOOL

Charles Drew University approved to start medical degree program by Marissa Evans, Staff Writer, *Los Angeles Times*, October 18, 2022 12:34 PM PT.

MEDICAL SCHOOL FACULTY

Ruth Janetta Temple, African American Heritage in Science, Engineering and Medicine in Los Angeles, *Los Angeles Almanac*. Accessed 11/16/2022.

Temple, Ruth Janetta (1892-1984) by DeWitt S. Williams, *Encyclopedia of Seventh-Day Adventists*, First Published: January 3, 2021.

Ruth Janetta Temple, Women's History Month Spotlight: Ruth Janetta Temple by Alana Reese, Uncategorized, Rancho Los Cerritos, March 29, 2022.

Dr. Patricia Bath, Changing the Face of Medicine, Celebrating America's Women Physicians, *U.S. National Library of Medicine*. Accessed January 15, 2023.

Dr. Patricia Bath, African American Heritage in Science, Engineering and Medicine in Los Angeles, *Los Angeles Almanac*. Accessed 11/16/2022.

Dr. Patricia Bath, *Wikipedia*. Accessed 1/5/2023.

MIDWIFE

Bridget 'Biddy' Mason, African American History of Los Angeles, Los Angeles Citywide Historic Context Statement, *Los Angeles Historic Resources Survey*, Prepared for: City of Los Angeles, Department of City Planning, Office of Historic Resources, February 2018. Accessed 12/7/2022. Page 11 and 151.

Biddy Mason, *Wikipedia*. Accessed 12/21/2022.

MODEL

Dorothy Dandridge, The Dandridge Drama by Mimi Avins, *Los Angeles Times*, August 21, 1999 12 AM PT.

Dorothy Dandridge, *Wikipedia*. Accessed 1/3/2023.

MORTICIAN

Long beach mortician will be first African-American female to open funeral center in city by Pamela Hale-Burns. *Press-Telegram*. Published September 29, 2012 at 12:00 a.m. Updated September 1, 2017 at 4:32 a.m. Accessed 2/16/2023.

MOTION PICTURE COMPANY

Lincoln Motion Picture Company Controlled by African Americans by John W. Ravage, February 16, 2007, *Black Past*. Accessed 11/16/22.

MOTORCYCLE OFFICER

Homer Garrott; Judge, 1st Black CHP Officer, L.A. Times Archives, *Los Angeles Times*, March 20, 1998, 12 AM PT.

Homer L. Garrott (1915-1998), Contributed by Dai'Quiriya Martinez, *Black Past*, November 22, 2017. Accessed 2/17/2023.

MUSICIANS

Henry J. Lewis, First African American Instrumentalist in a Major Symphony Orchestra, *Los Angeles Almanac*. Accessed 2/8/2023.

The Legacy of Henry Lewis, Los Angeles Philharmonic. Accessed February 8, 2023.

Buddy Collette's Los Angeles by Barbara Isenberg, Special to the *Los Angeles Times*, September 22, 2010 12 AM PT.

Buddy Collette dies at 89; L.A. jazz saxophone player, bandleader by Don Heckman, Special to the Times, *Los Angeles Times*, September 21, 2010 12 AM PT.

NEWSPAPER EDITOR

Robert Charles O'Hara Benjamin, R.C.O. Benjamin, *Wikipedia*. Accessed 12/20/2022.

NEWSPAPER JOURNALIST

Fay M. Jackson, USC BLack Alumni Association Timeline, University of Southern California Black Alumni Association. alumni.usc.edu/baa/timeline. Accessed 12/20/2022.

Fay M. Jackson, *Wikipedia*. Accessed 12/20/2022.

NEWSPAPER OWNERS

John Neimore, African American History of Los Angeles, Los Angeles Citywide Historic Context Statement, *Los Angeles Historic Resources Survey*, Prepared for: City of Los Angeles, Department of City Planning, Office of Historic Resources, February 2018. Accessed 12/7/2022. Pages 122-123.

The California Eagle: A Newspaper for a Black Readership That Was Ahead of Its Time by Kate Kelly. Black Leaders, Heroes & Trailblazers Archives, Only in the USA, AmericaComesAlive.com. Accessed 11/29/2022.

California Eagle, *Wikipedia*. Accessed 11/16/2022.

John Neimore, Not just along Central Avenue, but throughout...by Cecelia Rasmussen, *Los Angeles Times*, February. 22, 1993 12 AM PT.

Charlotta Bass, Newspapers, The California Eagle, Publisher Charlotta Bass. Produced by the *Public Broadcasting Service*. pbs.org/black-press/news_bios/ca_eagle.html. Accessed 12/30.2022.

Charlotta Bass, African American History of Los Angeles, Los Angeles Citywide Historic Context Statement, *Los Angeles Historic Resources Survey*, Prepared for: City of Los Angeles, Department of City Planning, Office of Historic Resources, February 2018. Accessed 12/7/2022. Page 122-124.

Overlooked No More: Before Kamala Harris, There Was Charlotta Bass: She was the first Black woman to run for vice president, in 1952. She was also a pioneering journalist. By Jessica Bennett, *The New York Times*, Published September 4, 2020. Updated January 29, 2021.

Charlotta Bass, Not just along Central Avenue, but throughout...by Cecelia Rasmussen, *Los Angeles Times*, February. 22, 1993 12 AM PT.

NURSE

Libbie Jennings Craft, African American History of Los Angeles, Los Angeles Citywide Historic Context Statement, *Los Angeles Historic Resources Survey*, Prepared for: City of Los Angeles, Department of City Planning, Office of Historic Resources, February 2018. Accessed 12/7/2022. Page 153.

Betty Smith Williams, Black Bruin History at UCLA, UCLA Alumni Newsletter. Accessed 2/8/2023.

Betty Smith Williams, *Wikipedia*. Accessed 2/8/2023.

OLYMPIC STAR

Valerie Brisco-Hooks, There's New Look and New Joy in Life for Brisco-Hooks by Scott Ostler, *Los Angeles Times*, January 9, 1985 12 AM PT.

POLICE OFFICERS

Robert Stewart, The Lost History of Robert Stewart, LAPD's First black Cop by David Mendez and Kate Kagle, Los Angeles, *Spectrum News 1*, Published 3 PM, September 27, 2020.

Georgia Ann Robinson, A Pioneer African American Police Officer, Crime, *Los Angeles Almanac*. Accessed 1/6/2023.

Officer Charles P. Williams, L.A. intersection named for city's first black officer killed in line of duty by Bob Pool, *Los Angeles Times*, January 16, 2010, 12 AM PT.

Vivian Strange, Historic Women Behind the Bench and Badge Los Angeles County, Crime & Justice, *Los Angeles Almanac*. Accessed 1/13/2023.

Vivian Strange, Los Angeles Public Library, Umbra Search. Accessed 1/13/2023.

Willie Williams, Los Angeles police chief after the 1992 riots, dies at age 72 by Joel Rubin, Assistant Editor, *Los Angeles Times*, April 27, 2016 8:26 PM PT.

Philadelphia Chief to Head LAPD : Police: Willie L. Williams will be first black to head department and first outsider since 1949. 'He's the best,' Police Commission President Stanley Sheinbaum says. By Rich Connell and Stephen Braun, Times Staff Writers, *Los Angeles Times*, April 16, 1992.

Ann Young Hits New Plateau in LAPD by Zanto Peabody, *Los Angeles Times*, April 6, 2000, 12 AM PT.

Regina Scott, LAPD Retirements: Three Say Goodbye, Dep. Chief Regina Scott; Capt. III Leland Sands; and Sgt. II Andre Plummer retire, Dep. Chief Regina Scott, Alive! News from the *Employees Club of California*, Los Angeles Police Department, January 1, 2022.

Regina Scott Makes History as First Black Female LAPD Deputy Chief by Jennifer Bihm, Contributing Writer, *Los Angeles Sentinel*. Published July 19, 2018.

Regina Scott, Historic Women Behind the Bench and Badge Los Angeles County, *Los Angeles Almanac*, Crime.

POLICE OVERSEERS

John A. Somerville, A Pioneer of Black Los Angeles, by Cecilia Rasmussen, Times Staff Writer, *Los Angeles Times*, December 23, 1996.

Marguerite P. Justice dies at 88; first black woman to serve on L.A. Police Commission by Valerie J. Nelson, *Los Angeles Times*, September 25, 2009 12 AM PT.

New President and Vice President of Police Commission Elected, LAPDonline. July 29, 2003. Accessed 8/8/2023.

POSTMASTER

Nancy C. Avery; First Black to Lead a Major Post Office, Obituaries, *Los Angeles Times*, February 2, 1992, 5:23 PM PT.

Leslie N. Shaw Dies; First Black Postmaster of a Major U.S. City, L.A. Times Archives, *Los Angeles Times*, March 10, 1985 12 AM PT.

PRIVATE INVESTIGATOR

Finding Marlowe by Daniel Miller, Enterprise Business Reporter, *Los Angeles Times*, November 1, 2014.

PROFESSOR

Betty Smith Williams, Black Bruin History at UCLA, UCLA Alumni Newsletter. Accessed February 8, 2023.

Betty Smith Williams, *Wikipedia*. Accessed February 8, 2023.

PROPERTY OWNERS

Peter Biggs, African American History of Los Angeles, Los Angeles Citywide Historic Context Statement, *Los Angeles Historic Resources Survey*, Prepared for: City of Los Angeles, Department of City Planning, Office of Historic Resources, February 2018. Accessed 12/7/2022. Page 10.

Bridget "Biddy" Mason, African American History of Los Angeles, Los Angeles Citywide Historic Context Statement, *Los Angeles Historic Resources Survey*, Prepared for: City of Los Angeles, Department of City Planning, Office of Historic Resources, February 2018. Accessed 12/7/2022. Pages 10-13.

Bruce's Beach, Newsletter: A century after its seizure, Bruce's Beach will be returned to its rightful owners by Gale Holland, Staff Writer, *Los Angeles Times*, June 29, 2022 6:30 AM PT.

Bruce's Beach, Family to sell Bruce's Beach property back to L.A. County for nearly $20 million by Rebecca Ellis, Staff Writer, *Los Angeles Times*, January 3, 2023 2:07 PM PT.

History made: Bruce's Beach has been returned to descendants of Black family by Rosanna Xia, Staff Writer, *Los Angeles Times*, July 20, 2022, 4:42 PM PT.

PUBLIC HEALTH SCHOOL GRADUATE

Dr. Geraldine Burton Branch, African American Heritage in Science, Engineering and Medicine in Los Angeles, *Los Angeles Almanac*. Accessed 11/16/2022.

Dr. Geraldine Burton Branch, *Wikipedia*. Accessed 1/10/2023.

QUARTERBACKS

Willie Wood, USC's first black quarterback and a Packers great, dies at 83 by Ryan Kartje, Staff Writer, *Los Angeles Times*, February 3, 2020, 7:51 PM PT. Accessed 2/27/2023.

Alexander: James Harris led the way for the Rams and Black quarterbacks by Jim Alexander, jalexander@scng.com,| *The Press-Enterprise, The Orange County Register*, Published: September 17, 2022 at 10:00 a.m. | Updated: September 17, 2022 at 11:25 a.m. Accessed 2/27/2023.

James "Shack" Harris: Pioneer quarterback for the LA Rams by Ronnie Eastham, Ramblin' Fans, Ram History, June 12, 2022. Accessed 2/27/2023.

QUILTERS

Meet The African American Quilters of Los Angeles, Road to California Inc. Quilters Conference & Showcase, road2ca.com. Accessed 2/28/2023.

RADIO PERSONALITIES

A.C. Bilbrew, *Wikipedia*. Accessed 1/6/2023.

Magnificent Montague, *Wikipedia*. Accessed 2/28/2023.

Magnificentmontague.com. Accessed 2/28/2023.

Brad Pye Jr., first Black sports broadcaster in L.A. and civic leader, dies at 89 by Emmanuel Morgan, *Los Angeles Times*, July 7, 2020, 9:15 AM PT.

RADIO STATIONS

KGFJ - Los Angeles, The Original 24-Hour Radio Station, The 1960's and Beyond by Jim Hilliker. Accessed 1/6/2023.

KJLH, *Wikipedia*. Accessed 8/9/2023.

KDAY, 1580 KDAY AM, Los Angeles was the first Hip-Hop radio station by *Daily Rap Facts*. Accessed 1/6/2023.

KBLA, Blackowned radio station launches on Juneteenth in Los Angeles by Lisa Olivia Fitch, *Our Weekly Los Angeles*, June 16, 2021.

REAL ESTATE MOGUL

National Association of Real Estate Boards, African American History of Los Angeles, Los Angeles Citywide Historic Context Statement, *Los Angeles Historic Resources Survey*, Prepared for: City of Los Angeles, Department of City Planning, Office of Historic Resources, February 2018. Accessed 12/7/2022. Page 43.

REAL ESTATE ORGANIZATION

Harriet Owens-Bynum, African American History of Los Angeles, Los Angeles Citywide Historic Context Statement, *Los Angeles Historic Resources Survey*, Prepared for: City of Los Angeles, Department of City Planning, Office of Historic Resources, February 2018. Accessed 12/7/2022. Page 16.

Consolidated Board of Realtists of Southern California, Inc. How It Started. Consolidated Board of Realtists website. Accessed 3.27.2023.

RECORD COMPANY

Sunshine Records (USA), Academic Dictionaries and Encyclopedias, *Wikipedia*. Accessed 2/8/2023.

Reb Spikes, *Wikipedia*. Accessed 2/8/2023.

RESTAURANT OWNER

The Legacy Of LA's Black-Owned Restaurants by Hadley Meares, LA History, *LAist*, Published March 2, 2022, 6:00 AM. Accessed 2/16/2023.

SCHOOL

Biddy Mason Park, Downtown Los Angeles Walking Tour, Dornsife. USC,edu. Accessed 8/16/2023.

51st Street School, Honoring L.A.'s Black Founders by Cecelia Rasmussen, *Los Angeles Times*, February 13, 1995 12 AM PT.

SCHOOL BOARD MEMBER

Fay E. Allen, Honoring L.A.'s Black Founders by Cecelia Rasmussen, *Los Angeles Times*, February 13, 1995 12 AM PT.

Fay E. Allen (Teacher), *Wikipedia*. Accessed 11/30/2022.

SCHOOL PRINCIPAL/SCHOOL TEACHER

Bessie Burke, First African American Teacher in Los Angeles by Cherly Tillman Lee (Family Editor), *Los Angeles Sentinel*, Published March 3, 2011.

Bessie Burke, *National Park Service, United States Department of the Interior* website. Accessed 11/16/22.

Bessie Burke, First African American Teacher in Los Angeles by Cherly Tillman Lee (Family Editor), *Los Angeles Sentinel*, Published March 3, 2011.

Bessie Burke, *National Park Service, United States Department of the Interior* website. Accessed 11/16/22.

Bessie Burke, Historic Resources Associated with African Americans in Los Angeles by Teresa Grimes, Senior Architectural Historian, National Register of Historic Places Multiple Property Documentation Form, *United States Department of the Interior, National Park Service*, 12/31/08. Accessed 12/7/2022.

SCHOOL SUPERINTENDENT

Michelle King is new superintendent for Los Angeles Unified School District by Howard Blume and Teresa Watanabe, *Los Angeles Times*, January 11, 2016.

Dr. Michelle King, the first African American woman to lead L.A. Unified, dies at 57 by Howard Blume, *Los Angeles Times*, February 2, 2019.

SHERIFFS

Julius Boyd Loving, Julius Loving: 1st African American LASD Deputy & Pioneer of Jail Penology. AV *Daily News*, Antelope Valley. Accessed 2/8/2023.

Julius Boyd Loving: A pioneer in correction innovation by Adrian Havlerstadt Director of Criminal Justice, Barclay College, The Pratt Tribune, February 9, 2022. Accessed February 2/8/2023.

Helena Ashby, Woman Named Sheriff's Chief : Promotions: Helena Ashby, a 31-year veteran, is the first female to hold that rank in the department. By Edward J. Boyer, Times Staff Writer, *Los Angeles Times*, January 26, 1995. 12 AM PT.

SOCCER STAR

Cobi Jones inducted into soccer Hall of Fame by Kevin Baxter, Staff Writer, *Los Angeles Times*, June 4, 2011, 4:24 PM PT.

STREET RACING

Man and myth, Part I: Uncovering the legend of Big Willie Robinson by Daniel Miller, Staff Writer, *Los Angeles Times*, July 9, 2019, 3:00 AM PT.

SURFERS

Nicolás Rolando Gabaldón, Riding a wave of history and commemoration in Santa Monica by Kurt Streeter, *Los Angeles Times*, June 1, 2013 12 AM PT.

A Former Pro Surfer Traded Unpredictable Waves for A Volatile Real Estate Market by Dennis Romero, *Los Angeles Weekly*, May 4, 2016. Accessed 8/8/2023.

Black Surfing Timeline History, A Great Day in the Stoke. Accessed 8/8/2023.

Black Surfers Reclaim Their Place on the Waves by Diane Cardwell, *The New York Times*, August 31, 2021. Accessed 8/8/2023.

TALENT AGENT

Wally 'Famous' Amos, How Wally Amos Made Famous Amos Cookies So Famous — With A Little Help From Marvin Gaye By Hadley Meares, LA History, *LAist*, Published Aug 13, 2019 6:00 AM. Accessed 12/16/22.

TELEVISION SHOW HOSTS

Nat King Cole, From the Archives: Nat 'King' Cole dies of cancer at 45 by Paul Weeks, Times Staff Writer, *Los Angeles Times*, February 16, 1965 12 AM PT.

Nat King Cole, Jazz Musician by Paul Weeks, Times Staff Writer, Hollywood Star Walk, *Los Angeles Times*, February 16, 1965.

Hadda Brooks, 86; Pianist Known as 'Queen of the Boogie' and a Popular Torch Singer by Dennis Mclellan, Times Staff Writer, *Los Angeles Times*, November 23, 2002 12 AM PT.

Hadda Brooks, Finally, Recognition for a Pioneer : R&B;'s Hadda Brooks Wasn't Looking for Fame--Just a Living by Don Heckman, Special to the Times, *Los Angeles Times*, February 23, 1993 12 AM PT.

TELEVISION NEWS ANCHORMAN

Ken Jones; L.A.'s 1st Black Anchorman by Myrna Oliver, *Los Angeles Times*, May 18, 1993 12 AM PT.

TRANSPORTATION EXPERTS

Lois Cooper, African American Heritage in Science, Engineering and Medicine in Los Angeles, *Los Angeles Almanac*. Accessed 11/16/2022.

Lois Cooper, Women engineers of the 20th century: Meet Lois Cooper, Institute for Transportation, *Iowa State University*, INTRANS, November 12, 2015. Accessed 1/9/2023.

Stephanie Wiggins, Metrolink hires its first black, female chief executive: MTA's Stephanie Wiggins by Laura J. Nelson, Staff Writer, *Los Angeles Times*, December 14, 2018 2:25 PM PT.

Stephanie Wiggins appointed as next Metro CEO by Leila Miller, Staff Writer, *Los Angeles Times*, April 8, 2021 9:09 PM PT.

UNIVERSITY GRADUATES

Alice Rowen Johnson, City of San Bernardino, Pioneer Women. SBCity.org. Accessed 1/5/2023.

Diana McNeil Pierson, USC BLack Alumni Association Timeline, *University of Southern California Black Alumni Association*. alumni.usc.edu/baa/timeline. Accessed 12/20/2022.

VALEDICTORIANS

Ralph Bunche, *Wikipedia*. Accessed 8/23/2023.

Remembering another UCLA Valedictorian by Brian W. Carter, Staff Writer, *Los Angeles Sentinel*. Published June 24, 2010. Accessed 2/17/2023.

Tianna Shaw-Wakeman, 1st Black valedictorian in USC's history, among Class of 2021 by Eric Resendiz and ABC7.com staff. Friday, May 14, 2021. Accessed 2/17/2023.

Valedictorian Tianna Shaw-Wakeman hopes to leave a lasting impact of sustainability at USC, USCNews.Edu. Accessed 8/23/2023.

VETERINARIAN

Rosalie A. Reed, *Wikipedia*. Accessed 2/13/2023.

VOTER

Lewis (Louis) Green, Voting, African American History of Los Angeles, Los Angeles Citywide Historic Context Statement, *Los Angeles Historic Resources Survey*, Prepared for: City of Los Angeles, Department of City Planning, Office of Historic Resources, February 2018. Accessed 12/7/2022. Page 15.

Lewis G. Green: A Pioneer of the Black Community of Los Angeles, 1850s-1880s by Paul R. Spitzzeri, *Homestead Museum*, The Homestead Blog, Posted on February 23, 2017.

WATER BOARD CHAIRWOMAN

West Basin Municipal Water District (West Basin) Director Gloria D. Gray Becomes First African American Woman Chairwoman of the Largest Urban Water Supplier in the Nation. Kimberlee Buck contributed to this report. *Los Angeles Sentinel*. October 11, 2018. Accessed 2/22/23.

X-RAY SPECIALIST

Raleigh Bledsoe, Kaiser Permanente, Who we are, Our history, Raleigh Bledsoe MD: First Black physician for Southern California Permanente Group. First Black radiologist west of Rockies. January 21, 2014. Accessed 2/14/2023.

Raleigh C. Bledsoe, MD, 1919-1996, Radiology, Published Online: Jan 1, 1997; https://doi.org/10.1148/radiology.202.1.286-a. Accessed 8/23/2023.

YOGA TEACHERS ASSOCIATION

A yogi's requiem by Gina Piccalo, Times Staff Writer, *Los Angeles Times*, October 23, 2004, 12 AM PT. Accessed 2/28/2023.

The Uncommon Yogi, *BlackYogaTeachersAlliance.org*. Accessed 8/23/2023.

ZOO DIRECTOR

L.A. City Council Confirms Denise M. Verret as Zoo Director of the Los Angeles Zoo & Botanical Gardens by Sentinel News Service, *Los Angeles Sentinel*. Published July 4, 2019. Accessed 2/13/2023.

Los Angeles Zoo & Botanical Garden Facts, Environment & Animals, *Los Angeles Almanac*. Accessed 6.23.2023

INDEX

ACKNOWLEDGMENTS

I would like to acknowledge my wife, Manal J. Aboelata-Henry, for being a lovingly supportive wife and creative thought partner. Thank you for patiently listening while I described each new discovery or repeated something I had discussed with you before. Over the years it has taken to complete this project, you've continued to offer your thoughts and perspectives. Thank you.

I would like to acknowledge my son, Tajuddin Henry, currently a 2nd year student at San Diego State University, for being a good son, for your leadership qualities and for using the foundation that we have built for you as a platform for exploring your interests and forging your own pathway.

I would like to my son Sadiq Henry, currently a 12th grader at King Drew Magnet School of Medicine and Science in Watts/Willowbrook and the high school valedictorian of our family, for being an amazing young man. By words, deeds and examples you have been a leader among your peers since you started in school.

I would like to acknowledge my son, Elias. You have grown up to become an honest, hard-working, law-abiding man who cares for his friends and family and I am very proud of you and the person that you have become.

I would like to acknowledge the *Los Angeles Times* newspaper and writing staff. Except for your reporting, much of the material in this book would have remained undocumented.

Last, I would like to acknowledge *Wikipedia*. It would have been much more difficult to find news articles and other primary sources used as references for this book in your absence.

PHOTO CREDITS

University of Southern California. Libraries.

California Historical Society

University of California, Los Angeles. Library Collection.

Wikimedia Commons. Media Repository.

Library of Congress. Prints and Photographs Division.

ABOUT THE AUTHOR

Randal Henry lives in the Crenshaw District with his beloved wife Manal and their two children, Taj, age 19 (sophomore at SDSU), and Sadiq (high school senior), age 17, at the time of book publication.

Randy was born and raised in Los Angeles, California. He loves the beach, views of snow-capped mountains, camping trips to Catalina, all kinds of food, whiskey/bourbon, IPAs, skiing, practicing martial arts (capoeira, hapkido and kali/eskrima), Kung Fu movies, family, friends and finding new things to see, do, hear, taste and experience in LA.

Randy has authored numerous scientific articles and several books including *Born in South LA: 100+ Remarkable African Americans Who Were Born, Raised, Lived or Died in South Los Angeles*; *Go Crenshaw: An Afrocentric Guide to the Crenshaw District*; *Go South LA: An Afrocentric Guide City Guide to South Los Angeles*; *C is for Capoeira: The Basics of Capoeira From A to Z*; and the upcoming, *Happened in South LA: An Afrocentric Chronology of 100+ Historic Events that Happened To, In, or Near South Los Angeles, California*. To learn more about Randy's publications, visit gocrenshaw.com/author-page.

Randy earned his doctorate and master of public health from UCLA and his BA in Political Science from Cal Poly Pomona. Prior to starting his own firm, Randy worked as a Senior Researcher/Administrator and/or Senior Analyst for the: UCLA School of Medicine; UCLA School of Public Health; Children's Hospital Los Angeles; University of Southern California/Keck School of Medicine; the Los Angeles County Department of Health/Public Health; and, the Veterans Health Administration.

Randy is the Founder of Community Intelligence (CI) Enterprises, an afrocentric health advocacy, education, evaluation, policy and research consulting and book publishing firm.

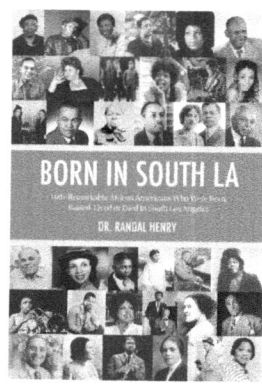

Born in South LA: 100+ Remarkable African Americans Who Were Born, Raised, Lived or Died in South Los Angeles is a celebration of the lives and legacies of over 100 African Americans from South Los Angeles.

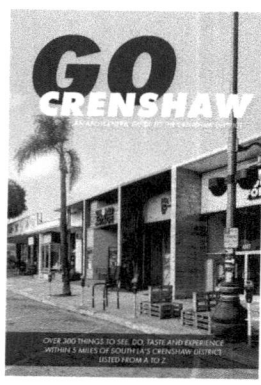

Go Crenshaw: An Afrocentric Guide to the Crenshaw District features 132 distinct categories highlighting over 300 things that you can see, do, taste and experience within 5 miles of the Crenshaw District.

Go South LA: An Afrocentric City Guide to South Los Angeles highlights the best of South LA's history, food, recreation, entertainment and services, helping readers discover the city from a Pan-African/Black perspective.

C is for Capoeira: The Basics of Capoeira from A to Z will help you become familiar with capoeira words and sounds and connect them to capoeira movements.